From Neediness to Fulfilment

to Fulfilment

Beyond Relationships of Dependence

T0159377

From Neediness to Fulfilment

Beyond Relationships of Dependence

Miriam Subirana

BOOKS

Winchester, UK
Washington, USA

First published by O-Books, 2013
O-Books is an imprint of John Hunt Publishing Ltd., Laurel House, Station Approach,
Alresford, Hants, SO24 9JH, UK
office1@jhpbooks.net
www.johnhuntpublishing.com

For distributor details and how to order please visit the 'Ordering' section on our website.

Text copyright: Miriam Subirana 2012

Original Title: Cómplices, más allá de las relaciones de Dependencia.
Translated by: Caroline Wilson

ISBN: 978 1 78099 129 0

A CIP catalogue record for this book is available from the British Library.

Design: Stuart Davies

Cover image: Painting by Miriam Subirana.

Printed and bound by CPI Group (UK) Ltd, Croydon, CR0 4YY

We operate a distinctive and ethical publishing philosophy in all
areas of our business, from our global network of authors to
production and worldwide distribution.

CONTENTS

Prologue by Pilar Jericó   1

INTRODUCTION   4
Relationships   5
What do we want?   7
My experience
This book   8

Chapter 1 THE CONTEXT   10
Commitment and/or desire   13
Together and separate: the image of the 'happy ever
    after' makes us keep going   14
At work   15
The search for alternative male models   16
We have made progress   17

Chapter 2 NEEDINESS   18
What else makes us needy?   20
Feeling the victim of your own doings
What is the desire worth satisfying and fighting for?   22
Need, desire, impulse or search?   24
Female neediness   25
The dependent mother and wife   31
Needy masculinity   35

Chapter 3 TOXIC MASCULINITY   37
Toxic channeling of the emotions   39
Emotional illiteracy
Profit for its own sake
Addiction to work   40
Risking one's health

Emotional disconnection 41

Fear of women 43

The transcendent dimension 44

Changing the patriarchal paradigm 45

Fatherless 46

It cannot be put off any longer 47

Chapter 4 RELATIONSHIPS 51

The gender equality discourse 52

Awakening from the dream 53

The hurt heart 61

Liquid relationships 80

Permanent dissatisfaction 84

What perpetuates this dissatisfaction in both
women and men? 85

Other aspects which perpetuate the emptiness
and dissatisfaction 96

Understanding the erroneous mechanisms we use to
fill our emptiness 97

The opportunity 99

Chapter 5 NEW RELATIONSHIPS 102

Understanding

Valuing and loving oneself: reality or mirage? 103

Partners, companions on the path, team, friendship 106

Agreements 108

Listening 109

Chapter 6 PARTNERS IN COMPLEMENTARITY 111

Identity 114

Female identities

Male identities 118

Chapter 7 PARTNERS TO LIVE IN WHOLENESS   121
Change your perception
Meet needs or transcend them?   123
Detach yourself and let go   129
Observe and revise   131
Renounce. Stop being the puppet of desire   132
Rebuild your own image   133
Love yourself   134
Connect to your inner power   138
Attention   140
Care for yourself and find calm   142
Awakening   145

Chapter 8 LIVE IN YOUR INNER POWER   147
The Goddesses
Opening awareness: communication with the origin 149
The energy level   151

Chapter 9 CREATING AND CONSTRUCTING A NEW
        PARADIGM TOGETHER   156
Reinventing ourselves
A mind capable of healing the world   158
Living in the being
A creative working world   159
A new vision
Bibliography   162
Notes   164

I dedicate this book:

To my parents, Juan Antonio and Mercedes, and to my brother Brian.

To Javier Melloni.

To Ima Sanchis, Joan Quintana, Liliana Maffiotte, Joan A. Melé, Marita Osés, Francesc Torralba, Eva Juan, Miquel Vidal, Pilar Jericó, Gaspar Hernández, Esther Trujillo, Josep Gajo, Xavier Guix, Bernardo García, Luis de Anta, Salvador García.

With them I have explored questions and new approaches for a life in freedom. My gratitude goes beyond what words can express. They have offered me their friendship with the possibility of seeing beyond established horizons.

To those who have shared their experiences with me. They have enabled me to enrich the reflections that I embark on here.

To the brothers and sisters of the Brahma Kumaris, with whom I have learned the value of an honest heart. Many of the experiences that I write of here are the fruit of my shared living with them and of having listened to so many women and men as they trusted me with their doubts, their fears and their dissatisfactions, their achievements and their yearnings.

To That One who is invisible to the eyes. He is in my Heart; He accompanies me with His unconditional love and caresses my soul in my dark nights and my days of light.

Prologue

In 1951 an inventory was made of the qualities that someone in management should have in order to be considered 'excellent'. Several were highlighted, such as tidiness, a well-presented appearance, or punctuality, although the most interesting one was the last, which said thus: 'Having a pleasant wife if he wants to be promoted'. Evidently, the possibility that the person aspiring to the post might be a woman was not contemplated... They were other times, of that there is no doubt. We can say that the twentieth century meant great advances in many areas in the West and one of the most important was that of women being incorporated into the spheres of social and economic power. In the past, around 4000 BC, the figures representing the Goddesses were of the same size as those of the gods, leading to the anthropologists' deduction that women played a leading and equal role in primitive societies. However, the climate change or 'desertification of the Sahara'—as Steve Taylor, professor of Cambridge, calls it—gave rise to, amongst other factors, a radical transformation of society. At a time of great shortage of resources, the need to compete for territory brought about power structures based on strength; this caused the apparition of patriarchy and, consequently, the relegation of women to roles that were dependent on those of the men. But all of this is changing. Today, the incorporation of women in positions of authority implies a deep transformation that is obliging us to look for new balances in couple and family relationships. The paradigms that our ancestors worked with are now obsolete, and to substitute them for new ones requires time and effort, on the part of both men and women, as can be deduced from the results of scientific studies.

Two years ago, *The Washington Post* published the conclusions of the analysis made by Babcock and Bowles, of Harvard

University, according to which the evaluations received by the most assertive women are worse than those who have a more passive role in a process of salary negotiation. They analyzed the opinion of men and women who had watched the recording of over one hundred negotiation processes with people of both sexes. Both women and men praised those males who showed more aggressive negotiation skills, arguing that they were clear about what they wanted, and they penalized the women who played the same role because they had been *less nice* and who, therefore, they would not give the job to. The conclusions are scary. Beyond the lack of work opportunities, it seems that a social prejudice or a paradigm exists in relation to women who are clear about what they want. That is why, if we want to change a situation that is so deeply rooted in our culture, probably we ourselves as women should begin to liberate ourselves from these toxic clichés, both in what we think and what we say when a woman attains a post of responsibility or, in the emotional terrain, when we want to live out a couple relationship as if it were a search for the handsome prince. We can blame history, culture or others, but I suspect that the work has to begin in each one of us, as Miriam invites us to explore.

This book is an invitation to learn to love ourselves and to love the other without engaging in toxic dependences, and without paradigms that choke us. It is an invitation to experience true love, that love which makes us free and that, as she states, 'arises out of the encounter of two wholes and not of the belief in and search for the joining of two halves'. Miriam knows that we cannot love if we do not feel realized as people; that is why she devotes her first chapters to smashing into tiny pieces the very real chains that imprison us. It is impossible to find realization in our partner if we are waiting for the other to rescue us; if we yearn for perfect, not real, relationships; or if we are so afraid of rejection that we drag dead relationships along with us. That is why this book is a navigation map for all those of us who want to lead a full and authentic life, not only in a partnership, but also in our relationship with ourselves.

A great essay—such as the one the reader has in his or her hands—invites us to think, to reflect and to be moved to action. To achieve this, Miriam courageously speaks to us out of her own experience, putting herself on the line and committing herself as a person, and what she achieves, through so doing, is that her words leave us far from indifferent. We have all been capable of living through situations of emotional dependence of one kind or another, and we know that, in those spirals, our self-esteem runs a mile. From those spaces we are not able to build solid relationships in which both partners grow in wholeness, because far too often we act out of automatic habit, unresolved needs and a long list of motives that enslave both us and our partner. Miriam shows us that another kind of love is possible, one which is born of wholeness, of the freedom to be oneself and to become a supportive partner on the other's path to freedom. Her book offers us clues of great value in the fascinating world of human relationships, navegation routes, studies that corroborate her words and accompany us on that journey which is always difficult but fruitful, the inner journey. It is a marvelous book, highly recommendable, brave, full of wisdom, of intimacy, inciting us to change and question ourselves, written by a woman who is a teacher in what she says, and, even more importantly, in what she does. It is a gift to be able to learn from her, from her friendship, from her way of understanding life and emotional relationships. Thank you for this gift.

Pilar Jericó
Partner of Be-Up and writer
www.pilarjerico.com

Introduction

Today we co-exist with diverse models of partnerships and family relationships. The grandparents—or the great-grandparents—who have always lived together. The separated parents. Young people who have brief flings with one another without commitment. Some people want to reproduce the grandparents' model: it seems more secure. Others opt for solitude as their faithful companion. Others decide to adopt children from other countries. Some bring up their partner's children. Others have children *in vitro*, with homosexual partners. Others decide not to have children or have them after the age of forty when they are professionally established.

All of these formulas open out in the present day like a rich social fan of different models of new ways of family living. In practically all of them, women continue to be the backbone, the fundamental axis that keeps all these new family groupings together.

These new groupings are making themselves a place in our social, educational and cultural spaces. Whilst as women we have advanced in all areas, men have watched, almost without participating, this female liberation that is transforming our social, cultural and relational foundations. In general, they have felt disarmed, not ready on an emotional level to co-exist with these changes which directly affect the sphere of the family group.

In a discussion group on self-esteem, various men confessed that they do not have problems in the professional arena, but that in the emotional and personal sphere they doubt themselves; they feel 'disarmed' and lacking in self-esteem. The self-esteem of most men is based on their professional achievements.

Another factor that affects men is that, in general, they find it difficult to be with a woman who is intellectually brilliant, highly educated, talented and professionally successful. For them, sharing life with a woman who has greater achievements and more resources in the professional world makes them insecure. They are afraid of being less than what she might hope for or desire, and of not being able to offer what has been traditionally considered the male contribution. They are subject, states Marina Subirats,[1] 'to feeling threatened by a loss of admiration or to doubt as to their own value and being reproached for their lack of achievement. Instinctively, therefore, men tend to make less of the positions reached by their partners, so that these latter will make fewer comparisons and demands'.

Taking this power game as a starting point, we need to understand the reasons that lead men to try to prevent or not make it easy for their wives to work outside the home. What is also the case is that through doing so they have been able to keep greater control of them. In the traditional social model, what prevailed was continuity, the children. For their sake, the woman subjugated herself and tried to keep hold of her belief in the handsome prince, in the king and protector of the home.

In these pages we will see how this traditional context continues to impregnate our spaces of relationships. In the chapters to come I offer paths towards reflection and radical transformation, from the inside out, in order to achieve a more harmonious co-existence. We will see how to connect to our essential identity, freeing ourselves from limiting conditioning, and we will focus our viewpoint and energy on creating bridges towards a world that is better for all women and men.

Relationships

At the present time it is necessary to strengthen a vision in which relationships can come to exist in a harmonious complementarity. We need a complete transformation so that harmony in freedom is possible. Men have much to offer in this. Without mutual collaboration and understanding, we will not be able to go forwards towards a true encounter with one another. Let us be partners in the creation of a new reality in which relationships are the expression of our wholeness.

Fortunately, there are more and more men who are making an effort to reach a maturity that can make satisfactory relationships possible. We should all of us, women and men, work to facilitate and encourage this change in order to eradicate the violence, the dissatisfaction and the insecurity that reign in the present day in all spheres of human life. For this change to be possible, we have to look anew at the basis of our relationships. And this reflection should begin in each one of us, in me, and in you.

If, for example, your relationship with the other is based on a need, on the constant search for gratification, you will also establish a similar relationship with society: you will try to get society to fulfil your needs and your deficiencies. The fact of relating out of need, looking to the other to satisfy you, makes it inevitable that there will be expectations, conflicts, frustration and a permanent dissatisfaction.

Then you feel yourself to be a victim because things neither work nor are as you want them to be. This causes a state of constant complaint. The universe does not seem to dance to your tune, your desire and your will. You hope for situations and others to make you happy. And since this desired happiness does not arrive—or when it arrives it dissolves as quickly as sugar on the tongue—the dissatisfaction increases in scale, ending up as desperation or dejection. You feel that you can't do anything to change what you would like to. You might also feel impotent in a relationship that does not seem to give you the satisfaction that you hope for.

In the pages to come I show the context in which our tendency towards dependence, and, therefore, permanent dissatisfaction, is generated. I suggest changes in perspective and attitude in order to achieve satisfaction, personal wholeness and harmony in relationships.

What do we want?

An important factor in connecting to our potential and transforming energy that would enable us to support each other in creating a new reality is the need to find out what our essential desire is. What do we want? What are we looking for? It is fundamental that we come to understand ourselves. Understand the self.

Who am I? What do I want? What is my identity? What is my will? From where do I act? From where do I choose? From fear and lack or from trust and abundance? Am I covering up a deficiency and am I hiding something, or is what I am doing born of desire?

What desire? What drives me? Are my actions driven by a mature love, a love that is worked at? Or am I seeking for the other to satiate my thirst for satisfaction, for pleasure and for love?

In this book we will see the repercussions of living in the paradigm that is based on need, on greed and an awareness that is based on what we are lacking. We will see how we can change to a paradigm that is based on the giving of oneself, generosity and abundance. Perhaps we should change the question and ask ourselves: what does the other need?

Rabindranath Tagore says:

I slept and I dreamt that life was joy.
I awoke and I saw that life was service.
I served and I saw that service was joy.

My experience

The women of my generation, now aged about fifty, experienced the 'harvest' of the protests and claims of 1968. We are the daughters of the generation that took up once more in Spain—in the sixties and the seventies—the feminist battles of the dawning years of the twentieth century. This opened the doors of freedom of choice to us. Many of us were able to study what we wanted, propelled by our vocation. We found work and housing. We traveled, we trained, we left the family home, we had male friends and lovers. We opted to do everything before getting married, and, even more so, before having children. We entered a working and intellectual world that was no longer the patrimony of men.

In spite of these achievements, we continue to carry a burden that is injected into our veins and our social fabric. If we understand it, we will be able to disarm it more easily. It is a burden that is so deeply rooted in our personality that sometimes we do not realize how our habits are colored by it. When these habits dominate our acts and feelings, we stop being the leaders of our lives and we live at the mercy of what traditionally and culturally has been considered 'right'.

Over the last twenty-five years I have listened to and attended to hundreds of women, most of them between 25 and 55 years of age. Women of different backgrounds, social classes and with different family and personal situations. I have seen, heard, and been witness to their feelings of guilt, their tendency towards submission, their destructive self-criticism, their need for dependence, their lack of criteria and how the opinion of others has influenced them, their clinging to power, their fear of rejection, their jealousy and their inner struggles, a lack of clear identity, a confusion and a yearning for a love that seems never to arrive.

I have felt how hard we find it to handle power from our femininity, and how we have come to exercise power on male terms in order to feel ourselves to be on the same plane as men. It seems there is a belief that thus we will be able to overcome the feeling of inferiority that has kept us in the shade for centuries. We find it difficult to balance vulnerability with inner power.

This book
My own experience of leadership in a religious organization that

is led by women but yet imitates the millenary male patterns, the female neediness of so many women and the present-day situation of lack of true encounter between men and women, has led me to question, to observe and to suggest new solutions for our present challenges.

It has all made me ask: is it possible to live without making demands, without expecting anything, either from one person or from many? We will study this matter in the coming pages. In them I share with you the results of this search for answers, in the hope that they might lead us to an understanding of the meaning lying beneath what is happening, and that we might be opened to new horizons, full of hope.

In chapters 1, 2 and 3, I write about, in a general way, the context we come from, what our history has been and the burden that we carry. We will see how this has generated submissive or authoritarian people and relationships in which dependence perpetuates violence and repression and prevents us from reaching wholeness. We find it hard to understand ourselves because we are living through a period of great transformations. And, in the metamorphosis, the chrysalis is no longer a caterpillar but neither is it yet a butterfly.

From chapter 4 we enter into this 'relational chrysalis' that is in full metamorphosis. What is happening in our relationships? In chapter 5, 'New Relationships', I set out the following questions: Towards where are we going? What direction do we want to go in? Let us be partners in this path towards living wholeness while understanding our identity. We will see this in chapters 6 and 7: 'Partners in Complementarity' and 'Partners to Live in Wholeness'.

Only when we live in our inner power (chapter 8) will we be able to create and build a new paradigm together (chapter 9).

Chapter 1

The Context

We are living at a time of confusion between men and women. Our relationships are unsatisfactory. The problem is not just a question of gender, but rather social, cultural and historical. It is a problem of disconnection with oneself and with one's essence. If I do not know myself nor understand myself, then neither will I understand the other. Out of this lack of understanding we find a mis-encounter in our relationships.

Dependent need, neediness, forms part of the culture of scarcity, of consumerism and of possessiveness. We live in a culture that is more about having than being, and what we have has a sell-by date. We yearn to have more and we lose ourselves in the anguish that is caused by the fear of loss. When we have, we possess; and when we possess, we are afraid of losing what we have. We consume a lot of energy in our desire to have, clinging on to what we have and are afraid of losing. We live in the mirage of possession, believing it to fulfil us and give us an apparent security when, in reality, it is unstable and insecure.

Culturally and traditionally, the female gender, women, had to be dependent. The aim of their lives was to devote themselves to others: to take care of them and to love them. They made the lives of others possible. Society grew from its most important mainstay: women's sacrifice. Their sacrifice meant that they could not develop their ability to make decisions, act as a leader, nor become a figure in their own right in the public world.

For centuries, this tradition has given shape to forms of personality and relationships that have been transmitted from one generation to another through some very deeply rooted cultural guidelines. The history that we were told at school was the history with men as protagonists, the victors or vanquished, conquerors, discoverers, princes and kings.

As a woman could not have her own criteria, her self-esteem depended on the men in her life, her father, her husband, sometimes her son, holding her in high or low esteem. For a long time mothers, and then teachers, taught this to little girls: her judgment had to depend on the man's judgment, therefore she could not have her own criteria referring to herself, on a scale of values, of good or bad; she only had to reflect the criteria of the other. The belief existed that to encourage little girls and adolescent ones to have their own criteria was harmful to them because then they would not be able to fulfil their role as women. This has been, and continues to be, in many places, the reality for thousands of women over many centuries.

They were so undervalued that their only way to obtain status was for a man, a 'superior being', to rescue them from their inferiority and raise them to the level of: 'You are my ideal woman, you are my lady, my goddess, my princess.' The typical thing in the falling in love stage. This lifted up a woman so much that it rescued her from her inferiority, because it was the man who put her on a pedestal. Theoretically, she expected to spend the rest of her life on that pedestal.

In exchange, the woman handed over her life, and put herself to serving him. This has given women the idea that the greatest happiness, the highest point of our lives, our nirvana, is love, understood as dependence on and subjugation to the other. Underlying this is the belief that the love of a man is what is going to transform you into a powerful being, given that you were born dispossessed. As women, our capacity to be loved has been fundamental for us to be able to act with confidence in society.

It may surprise you to know that the generation before mine, that of my mother, that is, the generation of women who were born in the thirties and forties, were obliged (in Franco's Spain) to do their Social Service, led by the Feminine Section of the

Falange.[1] Its objective was to encourage women in the national-syndicalism spirit. Its slogan was: 'The essential aim of woman is to act as a complement to man, forming with him, individually or collectively, a perfect social unit.' Its political ideology was based on promoting the traditional values which evoked the figure of the mother and the submissive wife as a feminine prototype.

Pilar Primo de Rivera, leader of this female social service, said in 1942: 'Women never discover anything; they are lacking, of course, the creative talent, reserved by God for male intelligence; we can do nothing more than interpret, for better or worse, what men give to us as already done.' And in 1944 this was published: 'The life of any woman, in spite of how much she might want to pretend otherwise, is nothing more than an eternal desire to find someone to submit herself to.'[2]

Young girls were prepared for marriage, since their purpose as women was based on being good wives and mothers. The advice published in the textbook that they studied sought to create attitudes of submission and dependence in relation to their future husband. For example, in principle 14 it told them: 'Remember that he is the boss of the house.' And in number 16: 'If you have any interest, try not to bore him by talking about it, given that women's interests are trivial in comparison to those of men.'

Being aware of what the generations previous to ours learned and experienced, we can understand the present-day situation of mis-encounter, in which all of us, both women and men, are striving to free ourselves from the burden of the past and to find new spaces of harmony and complicity.

Living in this socio-cultural context 'it is difficult not to feel ignored as single women', states Wendy Bristow. 'Our society celebrates family values and sanctifies the fact of having a partner. From the fairy tales to the television soaps, we are all delighted to see happy endings where the couples get married and live happily ever after. But the reality is not like that.'[3]

According to Teresa Forcades,[4] 'patriarchal thought constantly takes on a new guise in order to justify the subordination of women. Now it is saying that woman is superior—for biological reasons—to the male at love, which is the politically correct way today of saying that her natural place is in the home, with the children, elderly and sick'.

Commitment and/or desire

In the past, a man and woman married for life. There was a commitment. If this was betrayed, there was a terrible social price to be paid. So, **what came first was commitment, not desire**. Desire had to be deferred. When desire led them in a direction that was a threat to the couple, it had to be denied or destroyed.

As soon as we had a society that introduced divorce, this ended, because then separation was legitimatized. Then we understood that **desire comes before duty or commitment**. If your commitment coincides with your desire, fine. But when your desire is other, a conflict is generated. From here on, if the couple builds their relationship with the idea of 'forever', they live out a contradiction. Because there is 'forever' and there is 'until I want to' or until each one wants to. Therefore, it is advisable that an agreement be formulated and that each is clear about their desires, their intentions and their vision of the shared project that they want to build.

From there on, one thing is to live together, and another is to stay faithful. If they are not faithful, what happens? They promise, but nobody guarantees... Before, they had to do it, because, if not, they would have had the whole village after them. Now, if they are not, they might have some problems or an unpleasant surprise. They will argue about who keeps the flat or pays the mortgage, but in truth, nothing really terrible will happen. In the West this is socially and culturally accepted.

Together and separate: the image of the 'happy ever after' keeps us going

The contradiction we find ourselves in is that we still have the image of the 'happy ever after' when in reality the conditions have been set for a rupture. That is a risk for everyone, although above all for women. The woman who continues to believe that in order to do it better and give herself completely she has to renounce even her work can find herself at a moment in her life in which she is without resources, work, friends or interests of her own.

These days, men also face this risk. A man may find that, after working so hard to look after his family, the relationship with his wife sours, she asks for a separation and he ends up alone. He has to leave his home and, on top of that, pay her a monthly sum.

According to Mar Correa in her book,[5] 'the figures of the National Institute of Statistics in Spain suggest that around 400,000 women leave their jobs each year for personal reasons or to take on family responsibilities, compared to the 14,000 men who offer the same reasons for leaving their job'.

According to a study carried out by the Observatory of Women, Enterprise and Economy of the Chamber of Commerce of 2008,[6] everything indicates that one of the main factors that might explain the under-representation of women in managerial posts is the difficulty of reconciling family and work life, which obliges many women to leave the workforce or substantially reduce their working hours over long periods of time, making it difficult to acquire a specific human capital, or accumulate years of experience in posts of responsibility.

When she has made her family a priority and left her career to the side, a woman can come to realize that she has only lived through her husband and then, at a certain point in time, her husband breaks off his relations with her simply because he likes another woman, usually a younger one. This is acceptable to people, and considered normal. In fact, for a long time, it has been 'normal' for a man to go off with other women.

Women usually keep themselves dependent to protect themselves. They put up with things and sacrifice themselves. They make an effort to hold on to that husband. They do everything they can, they have cosmetic surgery, they make themselves up, they use creams, they dress in a certain way and do what he likes. In the Social Service textbook of the Falange that women received in preparation for marriage, principle 4 gave the following instructions: 'Prepare yourself: redo your makeup, put a ribbon in your hair. His hard day at work perhaps makes him in need of a bit of encouragement and one of your duties is to provide him with it.' But no matter how much makeup one puts on, it is evident that the husband might change his mind at any moment. This situation contributes to perpetuating women's anxiety and submission, especially if there are children involved and if the woman does not have an income of her own.

The acceptance of divorce has improved women's situation, given that the law protects them by giving them the right to a home and alimony for her and the children. Nevertheless, this does not mean that we do not feel lost, deceived or disappointed when our partnership breaks up.

Thus do we experience the contradictory anxiety of wanting to live together and separately, of wanting a lifelong partner and at the same time to be able to use it and throw it away afterwards. We maintain dependent relationships and at the same time we are looking for spaces of freedom. Because of this, many relationships are transitory pairings and separations. Love has come to be considered more of a connection than a communication or a bond. This way, partners become one more object for consumption.

At work

The nature of men's socialization pushes them to be combative, brave and confrontative. At stake is their pride and 'being a man'. In the traditional world, men had to fight harder.

For example, in the countryside, life was more arduous, the man was working on the land and returned home exhausted. If he had to go to war, he was really risking himself, and if he returned, he often returned wounded.

Today, being at the office can be tiring, competition is hard, but as we women are also at the office, we do not feel sorry for them because we know what it is like, we know that in many cases it is not so bad.

In the traditional world, the woman did not share the male sphere. The work that a man did seemed hard and tiring to her. She felt sorry for him, or rather, she felt gratitude or admiration, and this meant that when she gave him the best plate of food when he arrived home, or obeyed him, or took him his slippers, it was not only out of submission. The hard nature of his work made her feel compassion for him. It was work that in part the man did because he was also earning a living for her. The exchange, probably, was based on more basic things. The moment that women were also able to work and earn our living, this exchange no longer had meaning. However, both as men and women, we have it 'injected' into our veins.

The search for alternative male models

Patriarchal and sexist leadership continues to exist today in our society, perhaps covered up, but it is there. For example, Antonio García, promoter of the Men's Association for Gender Equality, tells us of how 'he began to go to schools to give talks and he realized that today's teenage boys continue to lack alternative models to those of strength, power, competition, social success, force, which represent traditional masculinity. Education is a key factor when it comes to breaking down the sexist structure which has known how to adapt to modern society, staying hidden underneath the false idea that equality has already been achieved'.

Antonio went through a personal catharsis which led him to create a men's group in Malaga: a space of communication and reflection in which the participants have to deconstruct themselves—changing their values and patterns of behaviour—in order to reconstruct themselves as egalitarian men who want to form relationships in conditions of equality. Thus was the Association of Men for Gender Equality born. He believes that the generalized vision that equality benefits women and is harmful to men has to be changed.

We have made progress

As women we have built bridges of liberation, opened up paths and normalized different models of family relationships; we have created new spaces in which women's role no longer makes submission to the male obligatory. We have created acceptance for women's vote, divorce, woman's independence, economic independence, the right to train in a profession, the right to enjoy a sex life not conditioned by marriage, and to be the ones who take the decisions about our lives and our body.

In spite of the feminist battles and claims, and the achievements of the last decades, there is still a long stretch to cover to reach a true social parallelism, an 'eradication' of male toxicity and the needy female. We should all be involved in this mission. Mariano Nieto, member of *Stopmachismo* in Madrid, states that 'to change the model it is necessary for men to be involved and engaged in a continuous self-critique, looking at themselves in the mirror of others in order to go forward together'.[7]

Chapter 2

Neediness

We live by cultivating a culture of having, overwhelmed by objects and material goods. A manager of the large department store El Corte Inglés told me that each week he saw the same people going in, taking home bags full of objects, and he used to wonder where they were putting them all. We go shopping without needing to, and we do so compulsively. We want to fill a void that we feel within.

We live in spaces that are getting smaller and smaller, and filled up with things. Small spaces not only on a physical level but also on an inner level: we have no space left to think in and in which to be able to feel from our true being. We are going round and round in what we already know, thinking and feeling the same over and over again, and there is no room left for the new. We lack the space that would allow for a flow of creative energy, and the space of silence from where to create and transcend in order to truly communicate and connect with ourselves and with the other.

Before our eyes we have a range of multiple choices that were previously unthinkable. At the presentation of the book *Creativity to Reinvent Your Life*,[1] Javier Melloni said:

Probably we have never had so much and at the same time been so dissatisfied. Those of us that have ever been in one of the so-called countries of 'the Third World' will have been struck by the happiness that there is on the faces there: in India, in Africa, in some places in Latin America that are not excessively contaminated by our western culture. The happiness on the faces, beginning with the children, is extra-ordinary. In contrast, our children here laugh little, and our faces normally show little light, few smiles.

What kind of society have we built that, having so much, we continue to be so dissatisfied; in fact, our dissatisfaction has increased? It is a huge question. And we want to transport our model to other countries labeled as underdeveloped! They might be economically underdeveloped, but in humanity they are much more developed than we are, who have a great deficit. **Humanity has to do with happiness, and happiness has to do with gratuity and with gratitude, that is, with the awareness of the 'gift'.** In sum, existence is a 'gift'. And if we turn life into a continuous expectation, a continuous demand, a continuous battle, our agony grows incessantly and untiringly, because there is a dynamic in desire that contains something that is always dissatisfied'.

On a bodily level we have some needs, on an emotional level others and, even more deeply, on the level of the soul there are others. They often get mixed up and confused. There are some needs that, logically, we want to satisfy, such as the need for affection, that of belonging, even the need to love and be loved. We need to have a place in the world, a mission, and to find meaning in our lives.

How can we satisfy these needs in such a way that they do not degenerate into dependence or an addiction? Is it possible to get out of the void and dissatisfaction that we are in?

What turns us into needy people? From a very young age we are taught forms of stimulation in order to achieve happiness, pleasure or satisfaction that are erroneous or deceiving. For example, we are taught to depend on external entertainment, on others entertaining us. We confuse the concepts of stimulus and entertainment with that of happiness. So we look for happiness externally; we want to 'consume' it. We are entertainment consumers.

We believe that with entertainment we will satisfy the need to evade ourselves, to relax, to forget or disconnect. The dependence on being entertained from without increases mental laziness. Personal creativity atrophies and we consume more external entertainment, becoming addicted to external stimuli. One example is the television programming, where game shows and competitions have a large audience.

When we require an external stimulus in order to experience certain emotional states, we are dependent beings. For example, if you like to argue because it makes you feel alive, in reality you are using anger because you are addicted to the adrenaline that it generates in you. Or if you keep on talking about what went wrong for you, what you lost, you wallow in grief and sorrows. We are using an external stimulus to keep ourselves angry or sad.

What else makes us needy?

The **ego** is lacking, it always needs and, therefore, it can satisfy neither itself nor the other. The ego causes dissatisfaction and pain. In the section 'Opening awareness' of chapter 8 I consider this subject in greater depth.

When our being has turned into a sieve, it doesn't matter how much we try to fill it; it empties. The content escapes through the holes. Complaining, criticizing and comparing; jealousy, expectations, projections, and other attitudes form those holes that keep us in a state of constant dissatisfaction. We pursue desire and, by the time it has been fulfilled, it has multiplied into many other desires.

Feeling the victim of your own doings

Have you felt or do you feel yourself the victim of your own creation? Did you create a family and now feel trapped? Did you build a house and end up being the victim of it? Did you buy an apartment and are now tied to the mortgage, or you sold it to get rid of it?

- Did you build up a company and turn into its victim?

- Have you ever felt yourself to be a victim?
- A victim of silence when you want to speak
- A victim of repression when you want to question
- A victim of wanting to be different and not being able to, or not daring to because of the fear paralyzing you
- A victim of verbal attack
- A victim of the other's misunderstanding
- A victim of interruptions that prevent you from expressing yourself fluently
- A victim of others when they don't listen to you
- A victim when you have to be somewhere and you don't want to
- A victim when you want to be present but you are absent
- A victim of the fact that you are ignored
- A victim of rejection
- A victim of people
- A victim of loneliness
- A victim of the body
- A victim of the mind
- A victim of beliefs
- A victim of the need to 'be somebody'
- A victim of being 'belittled'
- A victim of not receiving support when you most need it
- A victim of deceit
- A victim of order or disorder
- A victim of the established rules
- A victim of having to try to be something you are not
- A victim of having to do something you don't want to
- A victim of the other's stare
- A victim of...

So the question arises:

Who rules in your life?

You end up being the victim of everything that happens around you and of everyone that plays a part in your life, because you consider everything and everyone to be guilty of how you feel and how you respond. You give up your power to choose to external circumstances and so you become the victim of them.

You don't accept things as they come; you don't allow situations to arise as they are nor accept how others act with you. You would like things to be different and you put up resistance to them. Resisting consumes a lot of energy and it weakens you. To accept does not mean to agree. To accept is to keep your energy concentrated so as to create the right answer that leads you to the results you want to achieve.

If you keep believing that you are the victim, you cultivate a lot of desires for the other to change; you consider them the cause of your unhappiness and your 'victimitis'. Then you devote yourself to the pursuit of desires projected onto the other. Underlying this is the belief that if the other changes—and/or if circumstances are modified—you will no longer be a victim. As a result, this feeds the dissatisfaction and frustration.

What is the desire worth satisfying and fighting for?

True desire—let us call it the essential desire[3]—is connected to the desire for ecstasy, with the pleasure produced by union. We desire union, 'to feel ourselves at one' with the other, with the universe and/or with God. It is a desire that leads us outside of ourselves, where the I joins and aspires to a yearning for transcendence. On giving yourself over to the other, you transcend the I.

When you serve and give yourself to the other, you connect to that experience in which your I is joined and you become one with the other. Love and meaning flow. You feel the fullness of the giving to the other; you experience the pleasure of giving yourself.

When, on the other hand, the sensation is of separation, nonunion, absence or emptiness, desire arises. The search for meaning appears. You desire to leave yourself in order to reach the other, to achieve a union of heart, mind and spirit.

Emotional need hides the essential desire, the true need to fill an existential and spiritual emptiness. On trying to satisfy that emotional need through physical means of sensory experiences (purely genital sex, alcohol, drugs and other exterior and expansive forms that cause dependences in us) the emptiness is perpetuated, as well as being harmful to oneself and endangering one's health. If we strive to satisfy superfluous desires we remain in a state of non-awareness; we haven't discovered our essential desire, our deepest dream, our life ideal.

The relationships created out of neediness do not have a base; they are like a house of cards. One enters into a relationship where the heart is not present, only the emotional hungers flourish. They are relationships based on a 'fatal attraction' and on an intense desire that clouds the vision. Two people get together out of their insatiable needs and their neediness. They are in a 'hurry' to satisfy their hungers, their need for pleasure, and to fill the void of aloneness. All of this prevents them from seeing that perhaps the other person is not the right one to be establishing a lasting connection with or embarking on a family with. The desire clouds over their perception and they do not see the other in their totality but rather as an object that will allow them to be satisfied.

Sometimes they set out on a fictitious construction of a traditional family structure that apparently provides solidity. To this is added the lack of awareness of having children without maintaining a relationship founded on solid ground. Children suffer the consequences of this. They are born into dysfunctional families in which they do not experience acceptance, or the complementary maternal and paternal love. They grow up needy and hungry. They are children generated out of a love that is based on lack, an 'attachment' and impure love (with a mixture of conditionings and selfish desires), a palliative love.

The sensation of scarcity causes a state of constant need. It drives us to have relationships in order to cover over that emptiness, that separation, with love and with power. Love attracts us. Power attracts us. Without realizing, we fall into a love trap that is not love and a power that is not power. Finally, what comes is disappointment. We give ourselves to a love and/or a power that do not exist, that were fictitious. We lose the meaning, or, rather, we do not find it.

Need, desire, impulse or search?

Perhaps we should distinguish between need and desire. According to Josep Maria Fericgla,[4] 'desires keep us tied to the past because, in the main, they have come about in order to satisfy what is lacking from the past. Needs, however, project us towards the future because all living beings go forwards, have identity and discover the meaning of their existence through the path of satisfying their fundamental needs'.

Javier Melloni, in his book *El deseo esencial*, makes it clear for us that 'need is the child of repetition, each day we need to drink, each day, each minute, we need to breathe. Desire means newness and opening to otherness; it carries with it a principle of transcendence: to transcend your I, your small world, in order to open yourself to the other'.

In this book I do not go into the subtleties and differences between need and desire. I focus on understanding the state in which we feel needy, with the dissatisfaction of wanting, desiring and needing something that never comes. A state of permanent dissatisfaction, an emptiness never filled. In our search, we fall into the trap of the dependence that gives us the sensation of being full, of an apparent wholeness that is temporary and passing, and which, while seeming to approach us, in fact evades us.

To needs and desires, we could add impulses. These,

sometimes, are predatory, they arise out of our most animal and instinctive side, and they distance us from the intuition, which is more divine and transcendent. We could also differentiate between constructive impulses and annihilating and destructive impulses. Dominated by the animal impulse, you have desires that trap you by distancing you from what your soul really desires. When you live controlled by these impulses, you get lost in an earthly search, only connected through physical pleasure. You live blinded to spiritual reality, that which the eye does not see but which is felt in the soul and can be seen with the eye of consciousness (in the East this is known as 'the third eye').

When you do not find your purpose, you remain in a constant state of searching. You seek knowledge and beauty. You want to touch and absorb wisdom and thus raise your spirit to a transcendence in which you can calm your thirst and experience peace. When your search fulfils these requirements, it becomes spiritual, and you want to connect to the essential, shedding the superfluous. In the historical and cultural environment that we have been brought up in, both the male and female gender are conditioned by needs and dependences. The model that we learn to follow is deficient, even toxic. Let us look at some character- istics of male and female neediness.

Female neediness

Better to die standing than live on your knees.
Dolores Ibárruri

Female neediness shows itself in insecure women, with defensive and/or egocentric attitudes, who seek to reaffirm themselves through the other and/or material resources. Not all needy women go into a relationship out of passivity. Not all of them are submissive to the other. Some are dependent on and addicted to achievement. Others are addicted to power and to wielding authority.

We also see, sometimes incomprehensibly, that the generation after ours seeks to take refuge from their frustrations in old archetypes of love, the man and the traditional nuclear family. Perhaps they see the rupture, the instability and the torn way that children of separated parents live as a threat from which to run. This backward process may also be caused by the fact that women are living a limited freedom, together with the new generations of girls, who continue to live in their parents' house, unemployed, with neither economic resources nor the possibility of breaking away and flying free.

Marina Subirats tells me about the recent studies carried out in Spain on how young female university students behave and think and what their sexual relationship with young men is like. The results suggest that in the main this relationship is one of submission. Many times they accept sexual practices that do not give them pleasure but they do so not to lose the boy; for him it is so easy to change partners that they are afraid of ending up alone, so they accept unwanted sexual practices and the boy's imposition on their ways, how they dress, what they do, etc. Out of the fear of ending up alone, they accept submission.

Wendy Bristow recounts her experience:

> I know a woman who lives with a horrendous man, sexist and a drunkard, and yet does not leave him, in her own words, because she cannot bear the idea of spending Saturday nights alone. The fear of singledom in our society is such that it is possible that many women, on reading this confession, feel very identified with it and prepared to justify her words.[5]

As we see in the previous example, women have certain addictions that they even confuse with falling in love. We see other cases that Eckhart Tolle speaks of:

A woman who in childhood was physically abused by her father may find that her pain-body becomes easily activated in any close relationship with a man. Alternatively, the emotion that makes up this pain-body may draw her to a man whose pain-body is similar to that of her father. Her pain-body may feel a magnetic pull to someone who it senses will give it more of the same pain. That pain is sometimes misinterpreted as falling in love.[6]

We are afraid of loss, of rejection, of abandonment. We are afraid of loneliness. That is why as women we look for approval, to be useful and attractive. Being attractive, we manipulate and seduce in order to protect ourselves from these basic fears. We worry to excess about what others think of us. We act and say what we think the other person wants to see and listen to. That way we disconnect from our essential desire in order to satisfy the deficiencies and needs of others in order to 'look good' and 'be accepted and loved'.

A woman changes her clothes, accentuates her cleavage, plays the game of seduction, all to get back her control over men. Instead of caring for her being, she looks at her body from aesthetic standards. Our expectations, desires and needs enslave us. As Teresa Forcades states:

> Woman wants what those she loves want: if they all want to go to the sea, she won't go to the mountain, even if she wants to, because she loves them before she loves herself. Woman values the emotional connection more than her own autonomy. And if she is obliged to choose, she will always sacrifice her autonomy for this bond.[7]

'Love is woman's whole story, but only an episode in a man's,' says Germaine Necker. Love and giving are reflected on each page of woman's book; because in the end love is what it is about.

Sílvia Munt believes that 'as women we are always asking for love, because we were educated to. But, in fact, we all die in some way when we are no longer loved'.[8]

As love is so essential in women's lives, they become upset if they do not achieve it. It is no longer the anguish of not marrying; it used to be the anguish of the spinster, now it is the anguish of not having love. This pushes women to live out forms of submission, to all the aesthetic paraphernalia and anguish about her own body.

Sometimes a woman presents herself as weak and suffering in order to attract male protection and awaken his tenderness. She diminishes herself, she limits herself, so that the man is happy and satisfied through using his protective impulse. During a time of my 'dark nights', a friend appeared who protected me; he seemed in love and I believed it was so. When I left that time behind and got back my shine and potential, the man lost his interest in me and a distance was created in our friendship. In reality he used me to satisfy his need to protect. Then I found out about his history and I saw that he attached himself to women when they were in their 'low' time; when they got their power back, he would leave them. He constantly needed to be the protector king of the wrongly named 'weaker sex'. That was his 'male neediness'.

On the other hand, women also manipulate through ordering men around or through suffering. So, women have become manipulators in order not to lose their man and to have him under control at all times. A woman lives anxiously and submissively out of the fear of her husband changing his mind. It is the anxiety of not living love in trust. In female neediness, love is controlling; it allows neither the other nor oneself to breathe, which means that relationships that nourish mutual dependence become suffocating.

Women sometimes allow the other to take advantage of their goodness. Dependence makes it difficult to establish boundaries.

Goodness is a great quality that expresses beauty, generosity and good intention. However, when it is influenced by dependence, one wants to look good and please. This is why it transgresses one's own limits and lacks respect for oneself.

With all this behaviour and these attitudes, women weaken and damage themselves. What is more, they confuse men and cause misunderstandings.

We see how the romantic myth that we are a half that needs to find its other half still prevails, which means that it is difficult for the belief in 'Prince Charming' to die. This suggests a need for the readjustment of the female imagination that is very difficult. Although we say that we want to be equal, earn money and be independent, at bottom we are looking for a marvelous man. 'Marvelous' still means, for many women, that he is a success in whatever field he is in, that he has the biggest car, earns more money, is the nicest-looking in the neighborhood, the cleverest. That is, he is above me and that way he will protect me, save me and raise my social status. It is to reproduce the model of the superior male contrasted with the sacrificial and servile woman. Perhaps a marvelous man is really the one who shows you that he knows how to love you and is capable of living in equality.

Another manifestation of this situation can be seen in the women who **deny** their femininity. I am not referring to homosexuals, but rather to women who have interiorized the message that to be a woman is to be less. Like the grandmother Mar, who is now about seventy, and was one of the radical feminists in the sixties. She told me that she was the oldest of four. The other three are male. Mar got good marks at school, and the brother after her was a bad student. Her mother used to say to her when she was little: 'Well, this is now, but when you are fifteen you will stop studying, because at fifteen girls get silly; then your brother will study.' 'This,' Mar explained to me, 'made me say: "But what are you thinking about?" and then continue studying, studying, studying, and that brought about other problems because, obviously, what it made me do was deny my femininity, given that it was precisely my femininity that was going to turn me into an idiot. So, I denied it.' In order to mature and leave dependence behind, women should break with the image of the paternal figure as an imposing model that has not been understanding in relation to the emotions. She should go deeply within and become aware of her childhood traumas, of the fact that she has been dominated, oppressed and forced. It is fundamental to learn to let go and, thus, reinvent oneself.

Another important aspect to take into account is that, traditionally, our desire has been annulled; **we have been the object of desire, not the subject of desire**. Through not having been the subject of desire, we do not know what we want. I am referring specifically to the fact that we do not know what we want as free women, as 'Goddesses'. We do not know how to put ourselves in the place of the Goddesses and make proposals out of inner authority: that is how it should be. Instead we do the opposite: we ask permission to enter the male world, we dress like them (suits and jackets, etc.) so as not to be out of place, we talk about what they talk about so that they accept us, we do not have a fully developed alternative thinking.

In our search for meaning, when we find a man who seems to have found the purpose of his life we cling on to him and adopt his purpose without having found our own. Often his purpose is irrelevant for us, but the satisfaction that it gives us to live with purpose infects us and seems relevant to us. At bottom, we will continue to be needy until we find our own purpose, the life-giving project that will give significance to our life. If our meaning of life depends on the other, we will carry on clinging to him, since losing him would mean to live without purpose.

If we do not keep our eyes open or cultivate our inner being, the tendency to reproduce traditional and dependent behavior and attitudes will continue to control us.

The dependent mother and wife

The mother's mission is not to act as support, but rather to make that support unnecessary.
Dorothy Canfield Fisher[9]

The new female role offers a fundamental range of multiple situations. However, the connection between the image of woman and mother continues to be in force. There is a pattern that does not vary: the role of the woman as the main element in bringing the members of the 'clan' together. When a mother—or the grandmother—disappears, the family hub seems to unravel, the clan disperses, the family breaks up and it is difficult to stay close. It is rare, says Mar Correa, for the father to manage to keep the family united when the trunk, its foundation, its source, its greatest defense and its inspiration, is no longer there.

Society has assigned the role of emotional support of the family to the mother. This has obliged her to make great sacrifices, to rid herself of any individualism, in order to make others her priority. The personal, her time, her dreams, her freedoms, she herself, have gone on to a second level. It is evident that woman's capacity for abnegation, self-giving and sacrifice knows no limits.

Traditionally it is expected of the woman who is a wife and mother to be giving and self-sacrificing. To be invisible, that is, to make nothing of herself, silent. For everyone to feel good, thanks to her. This, luckily, is changing. It is particularly in the bosom of the family where the man has stopped being the king of the house and the woman has stopped being its servant.

However, women continue with their tendency towards dependence. Despite the changes that allow a woman to live as an independent subject, emancipated and with criteria of her own, women continue to experience an emptiness that sometimes leads them to have children out of a selfish need, to 'be someone' and to find meaning in their existence. Sometimes they have them in order to 'tie down' 'their man'. If they have a child with him, it will be more difficult to lose him. In those cases they have children not to bring a new being as a gift to the world, but rather for the child to give purpose to their existence and fulfil them. This also happens when the relationship with the husband is unstable and lacking in affection and wholeness. A needy and dependent woman keeps a husband needy and dependent and creates a child out of dependence. That way, the creation of the dependent person is prolonged, generating needy people, creating a needy humanity and society. A culture is cultivated of scarcity and lack: we are always in need and we never have enough.

Another situation that occurs arises out of men's emotional immaturity. As long as men continue to be emotionally underdeveloped in their relationships with women, they will often act more like a child than a man. Many women complain that their husbands act as if they were their children. 'I want my husband to be my husband, not another child.' A man who, in his professional, social and public life, seems resolved and decisive, in his private life and as a partner behaves like an adolescent. This is not a mystery, since men are educated to be men when it comes to work, sport, politics and sex, but they do not receive an emotional education so as to be able to relate maturely in intimate and close relationships as husbands or fathers.

If in the eyes of the man, the woman—his partner or wife— occupies the place of his mother, the man will start to look for her approval, or be afraid of her; he will try to impress her and will avoid displeasing her. Sometimes he will get angry with her for childish and irrelevant reasons.

The maternal behavior of the wife towards the husband will feed his adolescent, even childlike, behavior. Each one should be simultaneously responsible for working on themselves in order to be able to make connections as a mature couple.

Another direct effect of this maternal relationship of the woman with her husband is that the focus of the man's sexuality is not part of that connection. He will look for another woman who is devoid of all maternal energy. With her, he will have an ephemeral contact of emotional avoidance, a passing fling.

When the husband is an absent father or is not educated to communicate emotionally with his children, mothers cover over the void of paternal emotional communication by **overprotecting their children**. In this way, the male children grow up with this emotional dependence in relation to the mother. The mother who is needy and frustrated in the face of her husband's separation feels possessive towards her children and does not make it easy for them to enjoy their father. She enters into an emotional game in order to make the father suffer. In doing so, it is the children who suffer. Only in the emotionally present company of a man can a boy become a healthy man.

In certain Mediterranean cultures, mothers make their son the center of their life because the husband does not meet their needs. The marriage relationship does not work. It is the Oedipus complex: the son falls in love with the mother and it is a mutual falling in love, although often it is unconscious and not erotic. This happens during the three to five year old phase: little boys go through a phase of romantic love with their mother. And they begin to see their father as a rival. They will have successfully got over this phase when the rivalry turns into identification: the little one no longer competes but rather allies with his father. For this to happen the mother should not show herself to be more affectionate than usual; perhaps, in any case, a little more understanding.

The father should avoid authoritarian ways that would make it difficult for the boy to identify with him. Father and mother should continue to be as affectionate and united as always. If this is not so, this falling in love between a boy and his mother continues, especially when the mother and father do not get on.

When the mother realizes that the husband is not as she had thought, she tries to make the boy into the man that she would have wanted. Now this does not happen as much as before, because women also put their energy into their work and profession, thus feeling realized through other facets of their life, and have stopped focusing all their energy and the meaning of their life onto their son. In this kind of relationship where the mother is needy, the children learn that they are capable of influencing the mother's state of mind. Depending on how the son behaves, the mother is fine or not, feeling happy or worried. She is happy if the son molds himself to her expectations and desires. She suffers when it is not so. In the end, the male son grows up greatly influenced by his mother, consciously or unconsciously wrapped up in her emotional reactions and states. His relationship with women is difficult and he often repeats the pattern of his relationship with his mother in his relationships with other women.

In order to mature and 'become a man' he undertakes a battle to 'be free' and leave that dependence behind, pushed, in the first place, by the neediness of his mother. In this context, Sergio Sinay explains to us in his book *Masculinidad tóxica* that 'to "be a man" he should not fall in love—this would mean "giving in", handing himself over—nor should he tie himself to a woman, because if he does he would lose his "manhood". So the man, to maintain his power, makes a conquest of, impresses and/or submits the woman.' Which makes women more and more frustrated, more desiring of encounter and love, more upset. This causes an intensification of their desires and emotional demands. A moment comes when **men no longer understand women**: what do they want? It seems as if nothing satisfies them. They decide to put a distance to this "devouring" demand. The more distance, the more demand, and the more demand, the more avoidance. Men start to feel that women are to be feared. And women confirm that men are unable to commit. Thus, women and men dance in the shade, unable to dance in harmony together. **Each one feels empty of the other.**' The need increases. Anxiety and frustration follow it.

Needy masculinity

In needy masculinity, the man wants to be king. To be valued and appreciated. Taken into account in important decisions. He finds it difficult to go with the flow, he is not a good follower, he has the seed of the one who gives orders, he wants to be the leader where he is. He can't bear being dethroned. That is why he is competitive, needs to win. He needs to triumph and, if possible, become the best.

There are still men who do not want to change this patriarchal paradigm, but rather prefer to return to the old image of predatory masculinity. They are tempted to regress to a more primitive state as a way of affirming their masculinity. It is the dependence on the traditional model that considers the man to be king, the one who decides, who imposes, the powerful one, the macho.

Men continue to feed female neediness instead of meeting their own need. They need a submissive woman in order to 'be men'. In this way a relationship of co-dependence is perpetuated where the dissatisfaction gets greater and greater. They prolong and increase the need instead of satisfying it. Satisfying their need would be, for example, supporting her in her emotional autonomy and in her capacity for decision.

Men want to dominate the other person in order to reaffirm their own identity and worth. It is not a relationship of giving oneself to others but of using the other to reaffirm oneself. It is a relationship based on their own need. In consequence, that relationship always implies a tension, a suffering, a battle and a permanent anxiety.

Another aspect of male neediness is that men have a **need to do, do and do**. Why is something so desired? Perhaps to prove oneself, reaffirm and value oneself through this. Is this what gives meaning to their doing? In this intense desiring and uncontrolled acting, one puts pressure on oneself beyond certain limits, becoming stressed, empty, exhausted and without energy. The addiction to action empties him until his action loses its meaning.

His identity resides in doing; his honor relies on doing successfully. They are the kings of doing. When taken to an extreme it is a sign that something wrong is going on. There is no peace. The person escapes by fleeing from themselves, hiding behind uncontrolled action.

When he has problems, **man goes into his cave**; he does not do what a woman does: ring her friends. He feels that emotions can lay him bare. He does not want to show them. He is afraid of seeing himself as vulnerable. He considers vulnerability to be something feminine. If a man shows his vulnerability, he risks being called effeminate. If men do not change their patterns of behavior and free themselves of the stereotype that identifies them as men, many women will do without them. In fact, men have already stopped being necessary when it comes to creating a family. If they are there, fine, but their absence does not break the rhythm that women now maintain: mothers no longer have to abandon their working or social activities when a baby enters their lives, even though they might have to multiply their activities.

To reach this equality, harmony and complementarity, we have great work ahead. Women and men should accompany one another mutually to achieve a transformation from the root, changing the point of departure and the perspective from which we look at and perceive reality. Thus will we be able to get rid of the burden that we drag with us and see a future full of possibilities with renewed vision. We should get back our authentic identity and rid ourselves of all the stereotypes that distance us from the possibility of achieving harmony and wholeness.

We will explore other dimensions of male neediness in the chapter 'Toxic Masculinity'.

Chapter 3

Toxic Masculinity[1]

We inhabit a hostile world, full of injustice and imbalances, lack of respect, separatism and racism. An immoral world: bloody, corrupt, predatory. In all of this, the traditional male model has a central responsibility.

Today the male paradigm continues to be present in our inner and outer spaces, in our private and public life, in our nations. It has become toxic.

Toxic masculinity invades the world: wars, rape, accidents, death, obsessions with sport, social behavior, sexual attitudes, irresponsible sexuality, ways of political interaction, corruption, public discourse, the market and stock market, businesses without ethics, immoral consumerism together with devastating poverty and hunger, intolerance, fashions in television and film, competitivity, speed, predation, violence, multiplying addictions... All of this, for what? Are they ways of hiding anguish and the existential void?

Here is some data that confirms the toxicity in different male attitudes.

Everywhere in the world, many women die violently at the hands of men who are known to them. Thirty-three percent of the women who die in France are murdered by their partners, a percentage that increases to sixty-six percent in the US. In South Africa, a women is murdered every six hours by her partner or the previous one.[2] In Spain, 534 women were murdered by their partners or ex-partner between 1999 and July 2007. In 2009, 60 women in Spain were murdered by their partners (husband, live-in partner, boyfriend and their respective 'exes').[3]

In 2006 alone, files were opened in Spain on 175,000 men who had attacked their partners, and 90,000 protection orders were sought for women who put up with torture and aggression as a way of married life. In the second term of 2009 alone, 53,901 cases were legally admitted at the Court of Violence against Women, and 10,717 protection orders were applied for.[4]

In 2006, 17.3% of women immigrants reported an incident of mistreatment. It is also worrying that, on top of this, foreign women find themselves forced to withdraw complaints of gender violence: complaints that were made almost one and a half times more than by Spanish women. Of the 62 women who died in 2006 because of their partner or ex-partner, 19 were foreign. That is 30.6%.[5]

Many men die because of drugs. 83.9% of those who died in Spain due to this cause in 2004 were men. In 2005, it was 86.3%.[6]

The **salary of women** in jobs requiring the same professional qualification continues to be less than that of men. According to the statistical institute Eurostat, it is 15% less in Europe. In 2006, the average gross annual salary of women in Spain was 26.3% less than that of men.[7]

70% of the world's poor are women.

Sexual assault is a real plague on a worldwide scale, and it cuts through all social classes. The assault does not lessen for those who are richer or more 'educated'. Sexual lechery is a real enemy of respect and complementarity in relationships.

In many countries, television programs are a true breeding ground for the beliefs of predatory sexism. There is the attraction for speed, the man who conquers and triumphs and woman as an object of pleasure. Some of the language proceeding from toxic masculinity is used in films and in the news:

- Arrogance, force and power
- Abuse, mistreatment and aggression
- Compete, win and triumph
- Impose and dominate
- Pressurize

- Protect
- Provide
- Produce and yield
- Make hierarchy
- Order

Let us see other aspects of toxic masculinity.

Toxic channeling of the emotions

The emotions, feelings, doubts, fears, passivity, even the intuition, observed from the traditional male scheme of things, soften, distract, and compromise the fulfillment of objectives, jeopardizing success. Thus, we find that, often, the only emotions that men allow themselves are those related to lust and anger. The lust for power, sex, money and success. Through lust they attempt to channel the volcano of emotions that they have trapped inside. The result is violence and assault. War is the sexist way of conflict resolution. There are more than fifty wars in the world at this moment.

Emotional illiteracy

Men grow up and act in the world in an emotionally illiterate way. Man is emotionally castrated. It is thought that this is the way to preserve his masculinity.

The time has come to bring all this hidden world that is unknown by most men out into the open. It is a spiritual task that will allow us, both men and women, **to enjoy a whole masculinity, without masks, without violence**. This requires courage, commitment, compassion, creativity and wisdom. It does not mean becoming sensitized from a female point of view; rather for men to explore and discover an emotional model of their own. A compassion, intuition and tenderness that is male.

Profit for its own sake

Profit, money or power become ends in themselves and justify all the means. In this paradigm there is no place for compassion, co-creation and selfless co-operation: profit is an end in itself. This paradigm produces high rates of profitability for some and much higher rates of unhappiness for many more. It is a toxic form—physically, environmentally and spiritually—of working and doing business. It foments corruption, deceit, stress and a lack of health on all levels.

Addiction to work

Amongst men, addiction to work is not badly looked upon. In fact, there are companies who reward this devotion. One of the tacit rules of the male world consists of getting rid of those who do not perform enough.

This paradigm defines that man, and woman, are what they do. He is a lawyer, he is a businessman, he is a salesman, he is a footballer, he is a doctor. It confuses identity with profession. A man needs to be in the workplace to feel recognized. **When he stops doing, he feels that he stops being.** When men lose a job, they often feel that their life plan, their feeling of security and identity, is lost.

While men and women continue to be valued through the toxic paradigm, we will not go forward. This happens, for example, when a man who does not find great work or economic success is considered weak, even if he is a father who is emotionally devoted to his children, whose most important values are empathy, compassion, co-operation or sensitivity.

Risking one's health

This paradigm encourages selfishness and a lack of care. It shows itself in the way that men treat their health. Often, they risk their lives. There is a lot of data to confirm this. More men commit suicide than women; there are more homicides of men than of women; more men die in accidents. Many drinkers and smokers are uncaring of their health, and they make excuses for themselves such as 'you have to die of something', an absurd and regrettable saying. Sinay proposes that we change it for 'you have to live for something'. That we look for that deep 'for what', something that the sexist proposals are far from doing.

In the statistics of the main causes of death in men and women in the US, we see amongst those of men suicide, homicide and AIDS infection. None of these causes appear in the highest figures of female mortality. Sinay explains that this data reflects ways of living and of relating whereby violence, exercised over others, or towards oneself, and a lack of care, exercised over others or oneself, occupy a decisive place.

Emotional disconnection

Men often disconnect, given that they hide behind protective masks so as not to express their feelings. To open themselves to the world of emotions and feelings is more than a challenge for them. On having left their feelings outside of the life dynamic, they have kept themselves safe from vulnerability and doubt. They have behaved according to a role, appearance, their position, and not their being. In this way, man values himself and values the other according to the established parameters. All of this makes it difficult to create true emotional bonds with their children, their peers and the women they know.

The father is the absent figure. When he is there, it is difficult to establish emotional contact, or love, and to have him as a spiritual and emotional guide. If he is there, his presence is like a force of order that lays down the law and limits, not love and understanding. Paternity in this paradigm has many deficiencies. Man has not discovered the deepest, most essential and transcendent part of virility. He does not exercise paternity with understanding, devotion and self-giving. **The man who develops his paternity guides, supports, understands, nourishes, and generates happiness in living and feeling.**

Underneath these layers of external identities there is hidden in men a fear of true intimacy and emotional commitment. By the term 'intimacy' I am not referring here to sexuality, but rather to the giving of oneself in a space in which inner dimensions of oneself are shared, where one opens up and can thus express one's vulnerability. Intimacy facilitates closeness, contact and understanding.

With children, intimacy can mean a loss of authority (often confused with authoritarianism) for a man, which means that often in intimacy his doubts about what a mature and consolidated paternity might be reveal themselves.

Nathaniel Branden tells us of his experience in relation to intimacy:

> I remember my feelings of loneliness, on occasion very painful, and the desire for someone with whom to share ideas, interests and feelings. At the age of sixteen I accepted the idea that loneliness was a weakness and that the desire for intimacy with another person meant a failure of independence. I often identified the capacity to refuse and reject with 'strength'.[8]

To recognize impossibility, unwillingness and suffering carries with it the risk of being thought weak, lazy and vulnerable. Men do not slacken, they do not weaken, they do not cry, they do not complain. Men are not brave enough to see themselves as vulnerable, and for this reason they live in fear of the possibility of feeling pain; they flee from it.

Toxic masculinity drives out the harmony of opposites that complement each other. It generates duality. As Tolle[9] says:

> The force behind the ego's wanting creates 'enemies', that is to say, reaction in the form of an opposing force equal in intensity. The stronger the ego, the stronger the sense of separateness between people. The only actions that do not

cause opposing reactions are those that are aimed at the good of all. They are inclusive, not exclusive. They join, they don't separate.

Underneath the male paradigm, which rules in many corners of the world, lies the idea that all women are available to be used and, if they refuse, to be assaulted. So that rape is not considered a crime but rather a form of sexual activity. Men rape women both in times of peace and war. It is a way of controlling and dominating, as much in marriage as outside of it.

Often this paradigm keeps men angry, in silence and alone. Sinay expresses it thus:

Where women cry, men get angry. Where women talk, men remain in silence. Where women ask for help, men try to fix things on their own and however they can. Where women get sad and open themselves to pain in order to transcend it, men get hard, they close off. Women 'express' their feelings. Men, at best, 'talk' about them.

Is this constitutional of each gender, is it to be found in our DNA? My answer is no. This is the result of the application of the models in which we are educated.

Fear of women

Tolle[10] says:

Nobody knows the exact figure, because records were not kept, but it seems certain that during a three-hundred-year period between three and five million women were tortured and killed by the 'Holy Inquisition', an institution founded by the Roman Catholic church to suppress heresy. This surely ranks together with the Holocaust as one of the darkest chapters in human history. It was enough for a woman to show a love for animals, walk alone in the fields or woods, or gather medicinal plants, to be branded a witch, then tortured and burned at the stake. The sacred feminine was declared demonic, and an entire dimension largely disappeared from human experience. (...)

Who was responsible for this fear of the feminine that could only be described as acute collective paranoia? We could say: Of course, men were responsible.

Toxic masculinity conceived of woman as a threat. One had to 'defend oneself' from her, try to subjugate her or manipulate her.

Fortunately, in the last decades women have become emancipated; they have conquered professional, social and public spaces that were previously denied to them. This new woman is no longer easily manipulated. This woman wants an emotionally mature man at her side. This causes certain fears in a man: of not being able to be as efficient as he is required to be, of not being a good provider, not achieving the power that is demanded of a 'man'.

That is why sometimes a man, in order to feel strong, chooses a weak and uncomplaining woman who awakens tenderness and protection in him. That way he keeps her dependent while he feeds his dependence on being the strong and protective one. To do so, 'he comes to lay down his principles using brutality as an argument,' as Sinay explains to us;[11] 'he asks to be flattered in his mediocrity, he humiliates and tortures out of the fear that his authority be put in question, he wounds in order to feel strong, to be the "macho", in order to become a man.'

The transcendent dimension

In modern societies, religion as a vehicle of transcendence tends to disappear, at least in its traditional form but, for women, love continues to be what gives transcendence and meaning to life and, therefore, can lead to offering the marvelous moment that nothing else gives you. 'Love is the opium of women,' we are told by Marina Subirats.

For men, when they have lost the notion of God, transcendence is offered by success. That is why men are so insistent on the success that they can achieve by winning a football match, being a millionaire, or running faster than anyone else in the race, arriving at the end a second before, or patenting the idea before someone else. That is, triumphing. All the forms of competition that men invent are, at bottom, ways of satisfying the need for transcendence, to feel oneself above, to feel oneself to be someone.

Man gets depressed if he is not a success. Woman gets emotionally depressed if she does not receive 'the opium' of love.

Changing the patriarchal paradigm

In the last decades we have advanced in many areas in relation to gender equality. However, patriarchal leadership continues to dominate. The traditional mandate of masculinity, with its toxic burden of sexism, invades areas in which our collective destiny is at stake (in national and international politics, in business, in the environment, in the corporate culture, in the economy, in the development and use of technology and science, in sport). We are governed by the decisions of a toxic masculinity. It is toxic because it is violent, because it contaminates our spaces, because it causes significant imbalances, because it is driven by the greed that invades the culture of producing, growing, having and possessing, saving and keeping.

The consequences of living under this paradigm are present in our daily life. They affect our health, our relationships, suffering, the media, advertising, work and home places, they affect our economy, our sexuality, and, in essence, they affect our future plans and the possibility of a healthy future for our children and grandchildren, for ecology and for many species that are in danger of extinction.[12]

This dominant masculinity has affected women in many ways. Traditionally, women did not work and had to channel all their ambition for things, of being and having, through a man. To do this, they had no other weapon than to direct a man without his realizing, to get him to do what they wanted in such a way that the man believed that they were his own decisions, because if not it would be more difficult for the man to accept. In this way, women developed a manipulative capacity. As women, they could not get things in any other way, except through manipulation.

As women we are still emotionally dependent and we manipulate 'our' man in order not to lose him, so that he involves himself with his children; so that he does not get too distracted; so that he does not get entangled in things that are going to create a distance between us or that we are not clear about. **We confuse faithfulness with exclusivity, and love, with possession.** All of this consumes a great amount of emotional and mental energy.

Fatherless

Patriarchal society is, strangely enough, a fatherless society. I am not speaking of the absence of the father as someone who changes nappies or takes the children to school, but as **spiritual alchemist**, as guide and teacher who offers tools to transform the world, a desirable model of the world and who participates as a teacher in that transformation. A father who offers valuable support to his daughters in search of a partner. A father who is a point of reference of a new man so that his children grow up healthy and contribute generously to the construction of a healthier world, detoxified of sexist masculinity.

Generally, in the past, the life of a man did not change much if he had a child. That of a woman changes completely, given that she prioritizes love for her children over any other feeling, emotion or responsibility. Man has delegated to the mother part of what is his as father and point of reference. Sometimes it is the mother who takes over that space without letting him into it.

Whatever the case, it is difficult for us to find fathers who are reference points of a masculinity rooted in spirituality and a mature and balanced emotional life, freed of the toxicity of the patriarchal paradigm.

It cannot be put off any longer

For all the changes that women and a minority of men have brought about, male dominance and the toxic masculinity that has invaded our earthly globe lives on. The consequences of the violence imposed by the male paradigm are serious enough that we should not allow distraction, excuses or deferral. The change of the paradigm is absolutely necessary, a vital need; it is crucial, urgent, a priority. TODAY, NOW.

For this, as women we should free ourselves of the tendency towards submission and female stereotypes, and unfold our true power without becoming masculine. Leave behind dependent neediness and root ourselves in our inner power.

When as men and women we free ourselves of our dependences, we will go from being needy and lacking to being givers and those that bestow out of our inner values and our self-respect. We will rest upon our inner power. The challenge is great, for everybody.

Although women have begun to be admitted into the political, social and cultural fabric, we are in male positions under rules made by men and we act like them. We become masculinized. We are conditioned and do not change the patriarchal paradigm at its root.

As both men and women we should make an effort for toxic masculinity not to continue invading our public and private, relational and personal spaces, the corners of our being, our decisions and actions.

Women have shown an extraordinary capacity to serve and be of service. They have done amazing things. In general, they have not managed to make this into a measurable value for the

majority of men. They have served out of a position of dependence, with a generosity that has turned them into the victims of
a system. Men can effect a positive devolution and offer
themselves as part of the solution by setting out an integrating
peaceful model of mutual growth.

The attitude of self-giving is extraordinary, above all in
women. Men give themselves to their ideals, their country, their
work. This attitude of giving ourselves to the other and/or a cause
fills our life with meaning. In this giving to the other, traditionally women needed to see man as a superior being. Now we
should change. We have to be capable of destroying the idea of
Prince Charming and accept someone the same as, and even
considered 'inferior' to, ourselves. But they continue to be
external criteria (qualifications, professional achievements,
salary, intellectual capacity, etc.). The quality of the heart and the
values of being help us and complement us in mutual self-giving
and in complicity when faced with a shared project.

There exist women who have a strong capacity for emotional
autonomy. Probably there always have been, but in small
proportion. This is evolving and we find more and more women
with this autonomy. Today this capacity is valued as positive. In
the past it was probably penalized. The woman who took the
path of emotional autonomy received such hard sanctions that,
unless she was very strong, she had to correct herself and stay
dependent. In the present day, the woman who is strong and
autonomous from an emotional point of view is supported, so
that more women opt for this development, which in turn helps
them to move away from dependence.

We are living at a time of transition characterized by speed.
We co-exist with various models: those you inherited from your
grandmother or your mother, from your grandfather or your
father, and those you see in your daughter and your son, or the
model that others inculcated in you and the one you have
developed for yourself. This co-existence of various models

causes external and internal conflicts; conflicts between what is considered right or wrong; between what is socially acceptable or not; conflicts of identity and beliefs. We know what we don't want but we haven't defined the world that we do want to create.

Until now as women we have not had a global impact capable of changing the toxic masculinity that invades the system. The change that has been brought about is based on women being admitted to 'male posts' when this was not previously the case, but accepting male rules. This means a certain masculinization that has its positive aspect but that nevertheless is a masculinization. We have still not achieved true gender equality and for women's values to be considered as important as men's for the organization of life and the world.

I took part in a training course to encourage women to be the promoters of peace in conflict resolution. At most of the negotiating tables, for example, in the conflict of the Congo, or that of Afghanistan, only the men took part in the conversations. Involving women in the dialogues for conflict resolution would make it easier to manage the crisis, reach agreements that included all the people, and allow us to build and reinforce peace based on reconciliation and respect.[13]

A couple of decades ago I co-ordinated the international initiative 'Global Co-operation for a Better World' in Spain. We asked the participants of all ages: 'What is your vision of a better world? What actions are you prepared to take to make this better world into reality? What is your commitment?' We need more initiatives of this kind, which allow us to design a better world without the burdens of the past. The problems and conflicts of today's world are so great that many devote themselves to covering over the cracks and the wounds, and they have little time to visualize and design a future world in harmony.

To create this future world means to advance towards a gender equality that respects differences and welcomes talents, competences and skills without distortion. That is why gender equality supposes keeping some male rules. For example, the dimension of knowledge has been mainly male; we have absorbed it and it is of value. It also implies the incorporation of the female knowledge and dimension into leadership and into different aspects of human life. For a true equality, not only the relationships between couples would have to change, but also the relationships between communities, religions, political parties, countries and nations.

It is urgent for women and men to find ways to be companions in the creation of a healthier and more equal world on all levels.

Chapter 4

Relationships

Despite the environment that we live in and the burden that as humanity we drag with us:

> ... beyond the patriarchy there is you and your experiences. Your family. And the person that you love or loved or wanted to love and couldn't. Beyond the structural patterns of history and society's institutions are the concrete people who need to believe in the other, who dream of a way of living that is less cruel than the one surrounding us and who hope to find an intimate place in which to rebuild the meaning of life based on loving and feeling loved.[1]

Relationships are, or should be, a support for our life. Relationships mean, or should mean, an exchange of happiness and love. Harmonious relationships are the base from which to create, generate and carry out shared projects. Thanks to co-operation, we achieve our objectives.

When I have asked people in my seminars about the different factors causing them stress, worry and suffering in their lives, one of the main answers centers on relationships. Relationships have become a cause for worry, anxiety, being tied down and suffering. Rather than trust, what dominates is fear. In a love relationship—be it family or friendship—fear prevents the development and expression of all your potential, meaning that you stop being yourself and you are afraid of openly sharing yourself.

Due to emotional deficiencies and a lack of self-esteem, in order to learn to love yourself you need another or several other people to value you, to appreciate you, to need you and to love you. You don't quite manage to learn to love yourself and you keep depending on and worrying about other people's opinions, about what others might say, think or feel about you. That is why communication is fundamental in relationships.

Know how to express what you feel, don't create or believe suppositions, and clarify. When there is true dialogue we share what is essential and we resolve conflicts that divide us, cause confrontation or separate us. When the conflict is inside you, you can also find resolution in the dialogue between heart and mind; in the dialogue between reason and conscience.

The gender equality discourse

In relationships of gender, there is a politically correct discourse of gender equality that is generating, in the last instance, a society that is more and more polarized. In some way, we need to disarm that discourse, one that for many is a way of life. In the face of a personal conflict, they seek to come out of it as victors, and they join groups who defend their positions of confrontation and not of reconciliation.

Javier Melloni[2] states that the spiral of self-affirmation turns relationships into a challenge. The gender battle is one of the settings where the claims for one's own individuality can turn into hell, a long list of reproaches, aggressions and submissions. The qualities of each gender are used as strategies for control and oppression. The man uses physical strength and emotional coldness, while the woman makes the most of her emotional subtlety in order to manipulate and blackmail. The differences between them increase the disagreement and cause hate, instead of allowing for enrichment through complementarity.

'Whilst men fear women and women, men, it will be difficult, or almost impossible, for there to exist between them a relationship of recognition, acceptance and celebration of each one's singularity.'[3]

Relationship as a process of self-revelation

As long as you are using relationships as a means of gratification, to find pleasure, or as an escape route or distraction, there cannot be self-knowledge. You cannot know yourself in the mirror of the other, because you are using them to run from yourself or your loneliness.

You enter into an external stimulation that does not allow you to go into yourself. You want to remain in the known and you reduce the relationship to a level of security or habit. That way, the relationship becomes one more activity. If it were different, the relationship could be a process of self-revelation. That is, a relationship in which you discover yourself in the other and the other in you. Where there are not judgments but rather full acceptance. For this to be possible it is necessary to uncover mirages and demythologize love. To awaken from the wrong dreams.

Awakening from the dream

The idea that a person might be the remedy for our happiness, rooted in romanticism, is called to disappear in this century. Romantic love sets out from the premise that we are only a half and need to find our other half to feel complete. The new way of loving offers a new meaning, since it points to the drawing together of two wholes, not the union of two halves.

Undoubtedly, we should demythologize love. Some myths include the idea that love comes from without, that you need to look for and get love, that love is attachment, that love makes you suffer and that to worry is to love. They are myths, given that love arises from within and does not come from the outside and, therefore, we need to give love. Love is liberating and there is no clinging in it. Love is healing and, when it is healthy, does not make us suffer. Worrying comes from fear, but fear is not love, anything but. You cannot experience love and fear at the same time.

The dream

'Love is only a pastime in the life of man, whereas it is life itself for a woman,' said Lord Byron. According to Simone de Beauvoir, 'Love is woman's religion.'

Love is the engine of a woman's life, so many women claim, amongst them Mar Correa,[4] love understood as a generous, disinterested, reciprocal, serene and harmonious relationship, in which there is mutual recognition. Woman loves love, often more than the man who causes her that feeling. She finds herself in the reflection of the loved one's gaze, she grows, she abandons herself into man's arms, she gives herself; she makes love her source of energy, she feeds it, tends it and cares for it.

Woman desires to serve love, and that is why she sacrifices herself, she leaves her friends, leaves her work, moves city, puts up with disloyalties, complies with what is asked of her, limits her freedoms; all that is hers passes onto a second plane for the good of her loved one's happiness. Woman desires to feel herself beautiful, useful, necessary, indispensable, unique to the man in love, whom she elevates, admires and adores. She lives for and by love; she feeds off it, off the happiness and suffering that it sometimes causes her. Her true vocation is to feel herself in love, and for this she will set aside her own autonomy so as to give herself in body and soul to the loved one.

'Even though we are aware that we are making a mistake,' says Correa, 'although we know it will bring us pain, although each time it is more difficult to recover, a woman's giving of herself to love continues to be total and absolute, blind and generous, universal.'

The stage of being in love is a founding moment of love. When it has enough importance for both to be thinking of a long time of living together and forming a family, this premise founded on and inundated by love carries great weight. So much so, that the woman believes that this will last and turns that man into the ideal Prince Charming onto whom she projects all her dreams.

Later, many times, reality will show her that it was not really the case. Then, there are two reactions. Previously, in most traditional relationships, as there was no room for separation, the reaction was one of resignation. Nowadays, separation is the usual reaction. Although, due to the crisis, there are couples who cannot afford the cost of separation and resign themselves to living together but separately.

Marina Subirats told me an anecdote that seemed extraordinary to her. A woman explained to her: 'I have my husband as if on a pedestal above the bed and every day, when he returns at night, this little statue falls and breaks into pieces, but the next day, I pick it up, stick it back together, and put it back on the pedestal.' It seems to me a frequent operation amongst women, says Subirats. Traditionally, a woman had to live with whatever there was, even if the man was violent and hit her. To bear it, she needed to keep believing in that superior man. In a woman's imagination even the blows were justified. That is the origin of the thought: 'I must have done something; maybe I deserve it', words heard so often in interviews with women who have been hit: 'You see, perhaps I deserved it.' They look for excuses in order to keep their man on the pedestal and to be able to bear the situation.

If he falls definitively off the pedestal and you can't stick him back together, your life would be wasted: you would be wasting it at the side of someone not worth it; for him to be worth it, this non-existent Prince Charming has to be constantly reconstructed.

With this behavior, women end up harming themselves. Nevertheless, traditionally, it used to mean more harm for the woman if she left—because if she broke up the marriage she was despised. Often her family would not recognize her, she had no money, she lost her children; it was a loss in many senses. The only way to conserve a socially acceptable situation was to put up with it.

Despite all the changes we have achieved in past decades, a majority of people continue to associate marriage with stability, having a partner with happiness, love with fidelity, maternity with fulfillment. Thus, many young women want to return into that fatal trap for women's autonomy, believing that it is the only way possible to develop socially, emotionally, economically, sexually and inwardly.

It seems that the dream of Prince Charming has not yet died. In our childhood we dreamed of one day marrying a marvelous man who would love us eternally. We played at princes and princesses. I loved playing at princesses, in the playground at the Talitha School (later the Orlandai School). With the other little girls I built castles amongst the trees in the garden and from there we visualized our prince. We imagined our happy home. Today I watch with surprise at how little girls and boys talk about girlfriends and boyfriends. As if this was what life is about: about finding a boyfriend, finding your Prince Charming or your Cinderella and living happily ever after. We continue to transmit this dream from generation to generation.

We grow up as women holding on to a dream. You dream of Prince Charming appearing in your life. When a man appears, you turn him into an actor in the script of your dream. As you are building the dream, you receive signs that he isn't this, but you don't listen to them. What he tells you or does, you adapt to your dream, you 'rewrite it', you reinterpret it. You don't listen objectively or clearly. You pick up on the signals but you pay them no heed. You want to live out your dream. It is the most important thing to you. If there is sex in the relationship as well, it becomes even more difficult to realize, because sex satisfies a need of yours, a pleasure and so you give in. He is how he is, but you don't see it because you reinterpret his attitudes, words and actions to make them fit into your dream.

The man also has to open himself in order to differentiate the woman he has before him or at his side from the one he has interiorized in his mind and/or his heart. That requires emotional and spiritual courage. Knowing how to see, listen, understand and be in harmony with the other. Listening to the signals that point to the differences between what you imagine and who the other really is.

The blow

When you finally listen to the signals, you experience a disappointment. As a result there is a lot of grief and sadness. You go through an inner battle. You turned the man or the woman into part of your dream. He or she has been like they were all along, but you didn't want to take it on board. You didn't want to see the reality. You didn't want to differentiate the real man or woman from the man or woman that you internalized in your mind: they are not the same.

The dream of Prince Charming collapses because he never existed. When he has fallen off the pedestal you have set him on, the blow is devastating. Your expectations have led you to feel totally taken in. Paradoxically, it upsets you, as a woman, because he gets himself up to look for another heart to conquer, another territory to reign over. It also happens the other way round.

The pedestal has broken and he is not there any more.

You feel that the floor has given way under your feet, that you are falling into a huge pit that seems to have no bottom. You feel frustration, bitterness, indignation, anger, and a sharp and stabbing pain that you start to think will never leave you. The suffering is terrible when you see blasted into nothing a life project that you poured so much passion into, where you deposited the best years of your life, that you had believed so much in, on which you had built your own and your children's happiness.[5]

Then the reproaches begin, the bad temper, the conflicts between what has been, what is and how you would like it to be. Your confidence is shattered. You feel the failure of your emotional project, the other's ingratitude towards you and your giving, and anger about everything that is happening.

It is not only the man who breaks up a marriage by going off with another woman (prettier, younger, more submissive); this can also happen to the man when he is rejected by a woman, the mother of his children. It is not necessarily because she goes off with another man. The woman accumulates anger inside because things are not as she would like them to be. In the end the anger makes her intolerant, sad, bad-tempered, and she decides that the solution lies in 'getting rid of' the man who apparently causes all these bad feelings and is the cause of all the reproaches. Generally, the woman feels dissatisfied because that fusion of being in love disappears. She tries to rebuild and re-find it. She tries to exchange sex for intimacy, understanding emotional fusion as intimacy. But true fusion does not take place physically. It is a matter of entering into the mature spiritual and emotional dimension in which soul, mind and body are absorbed in that experience. We will explore this in the pages to come.

The point of departure

Relating from what 'you need', from your limited self, will lead you to dependence, to suffering and to getting more deeply involved in an unsustainable relationship.

As men and women we have needs and dependences. If we realize what ours are and what the other's are, we will protect ourselves and we will be wiser in the relationship so as not to use the other simply to satisfy ourselves. That way we won't fall into disappointment or deceit. The woman should see and be aware of the man's need, male neediness, and so will not feel taken in. The woman allows herself to be trapped in this deception because she is usually more emotionally dependent. She lowers her standards in order to meet her emotional need for belonging.

The need to belong is universal. We want to belong to a group, a collective, a clan, a family, a club, a race, a team, etc. Before belonging to another you have to belong to yourself. As a woman, be your own owner. As a man, you should also walk this path given that, generally, men belong to their ideas and/or their work or professional project before belonging to themselves. Women have copied that paradigm of masculinity and ended up belonging to work, their ideas, be they feminists, politicians or religious women, before belonging to themselves. Belonging to yourself means that you are the owner of your mind, your heart and your body. You are the ruler of all your being: of what you think and feel. Being the owner of yourself means that, when you give yourself to an ideal, a person, a cause, you don't do so by denying or sacrificing yourself. You stay faithful to yourself by holding onto the reins of your life.

Being in love

Being in love for a man is the same as giving himself up, a difficult state for him to maintain, given what this means in a system of thought developed upon concepts such as fight, competition, victory, conquest, imposition and possession. Women are 'conquered'. A man in love is a man given over. This, in the traditional male mandate, is not allowed. It means to be 'weak', allowing oneself to be influenced and losing control.

So, we see that men 'like' women. Women 'fall in love' with men. He desires her; she loves him. Sinay asks the following question: 'Is it naturally like that?'. His answer is no. It is the result of an education, of rules and of a paradigm.

For men, being in love is a parenthesis. The mandate for them, according to traditional cultural stereotypes, is that the male should be strong and not carried away by his feelings, able to control them, even be above them, and doing what he has to do. This is what traditional patriotic, cultural or economic duties have demanded. All of this is changing.

In general, the only socially acceptable moment for men to be sensitive and allow themselves to be carried away by feeling is the moment of falling in love. There they play this role and women interpret it as if it was forever; the dream awakens in them. It might even be that it is forever in the imagination of both of them. Men are changing a little now, as they know that there are more break-ups. This commitment is more difficult for them. They have more brief affairs than fallings in love.

It is possible that in most people's life there is some period of being or falling in love. Not all forms of partnership are destined at that moment to last over time. Probably, the men that establish such connections are not ready to go so far in many cases. They begin the relationship thinking that it is a brief fling or a temporary connection.

In a woman's imagination, it is not usually like that. The desire to belong and for security feeds the hope of a lasting relationship, although this is also changing and some women do not want to 'tie themselves down' either. When asked, some adolescent girls say: 'I am not going to get married, I am not going to have children.' What they do not give up on is the moment of romanticism that for them is the full moon, the beach, a man in love, a song. It is a stereotype that women are not willing to give up.

Both as men and women we should become aware of our deficiencies and the games we fall into in order to satisfy them. They are games that have a mental, emotional and physical cost. Generally a woman feels attracted and gives herself honestly, but she is capable of sacrificing, diminishing and submitting herself. The man usually uses this attraction of hers to satisfy his own needs selfishly. The reverse also happens, when women emotionally manipulate men. All this leaves us with a hurt heart. We need to get out of this spiral of dependent neediness, attachment, rupture, loss, anger, frustration and sadness. To do so we need a light that allows us to wake up.

The hurt heart

A hurt heart does not manage the emotions well. It protects itself from fear and, paradoxically, it fears protection. When it feels caged in, it rejects this protection and fears it. From feeling protected to feeling caged in there is a fine line, a small step.

Feelings get mixed up where suffering compromises the soul. Good decisions are not made. One doesn't think clearly. Grief is mixed with anger. Frustration with hate. Impatience with rejection.

We do not want to live hardened, without heart. Living with our heart hidden, protected by a system of self-defense, makes us insensitive and blocks our energy of love.

According to Sergio Sinay, in the face of few kinds of pain is a man so disarmed, so stripped of resources as in when faced with abandonment by a woman. It is an unbearable failure for the man – to be abandoned by a woman. It makes him feel a complete 'loser' (he loses her and he loses in front of her).

Let us learn to manage suffering, to accept it, look it in the face and be able to let go of it. If we flee from it, it pursues us. The suffering of the heart shows itself in different ways. Let us look at some of them and how to manage them.

Disappointment

You feel disappointed. The person has not been nor is as you were hoping. The relationship has broken up. The project has come to a halt. You have woken up from the dream. You become aware of all the signals that you received on the path that were pointing out to you that the truth wasn't going in that direction, signals that you ignored. You were clinging on to the dream. Now you have woken up and you are deeply disappointed. It seems as if your life has lost meaning. Everything that you built with your best intentions, energies and passions seems to have vanished into the air. Disappointment floods you and you feel weak. You seem to have lost your way and no longer know where you are going.

All your effort has not been in vain. The time has come to stop, create and reinvent your life. You may feel the desire to run, to find distraction, keep yourself busy so as not to feel the suffering. However, only through facing it will you be able to let it go. Hiding it, you will feel it in your body, and it will affect your emotional, mental and physical health. If you justify yourself or blame yourself you will not heal it.

The disappointment that comes from disloyalty and feeling betrayed is a difficult abyss to cross. The betrayal of what you have believed in, trusted in and fought for, is a hard blow. We ought to look at how each person defines, understands and speaks of betrayal and disloyalty. The perception and the telling are different for everyone. The important thing is not to fall into the temptation of blaming the other one, hating them and projecting onto him or her all the causes of your disappointment. What is disloyalty or betrayal for one person for someone else is liberation and honesty. Simply, their different points of view have not been shared and there is neither understanding nor communication. One justifies themselves in their deep pain of a broken dream, for a feeling of betrayal that has shattered the trust.

However, if you could raise your sights beyond your home, your village or your town, your country, and see the world for the marvelous earthly globe that it is, you would realize that in reality what has happened was insignificant. Life goes on, in constant change. Do not allow your mind to get obsessed and your heart to stay stuck in what has happened. If you really want to free yourself, don't seek revenge. Think that everything is a great cosmic play.

To recover from the inner wounds and a spirit that seems devastated, nurture your priorities and release yourself from the yoke of the tie that there was or the weight of a broken relationship. What is the priority now: to remake your life or stay stuck in the past? The past is one of the greatest attachments we have.

In the face of disappointment, the solution is acceptance and forgiveness. Accepting what has happened. Accepting that you believed in it and it wasn't thus. Accepting your mistake and/or that of the other. Forgiving yourself. Forgive. This will open the doors to healing the hurt heart.

To do so, you should get back your mastery over your mind: your thoughts. Without this control, your mind will go back again and again to that place of suffering; it will repeat the 'why me? How dare they?' And, like a constant hammering, it will go on lowering your self-esteem and the bedrock of your inner power. Like woodworm, your own thought will make holes in your inner being and you will stay empty, without energy. What you think has a connection to the results you get. But when you say: 'You make me feel like that, you make me sad, why did you do that to me?', you show that you are not aware of this connection. It is as if in that moment you were asleep or uncon-scious. You have forgotten the first principle of self-leadership: nobody creates your thoughts or feeling except you yourself.

Practical advice: think positively; you are the creator of your thoughts. Meditate. Forgive and let go. Look forward.

Sadness

Have such powerful thoughts that each scene of life that takes place really stays behind, instead of remaining rooted in your thoughts.
Dadi Janki

Sadness arises out of the feeling of loss that leaves us in a void. The void of love's loss is devastating. It produces a sadness that seems inconsolable. It takes up every part of your being. All of you is sadness.

By crying over the past you fix nothing. Open yourself to forgiveness. Raise the level of your thoughts so that they do not keep you in a state of sadness and loss of hope. Focus your eyes on the present and the future, so that your energy can flow again. Love continues in you. You are love and you can continue to irradiate it. Discover it. When you possess you can lose, and when you lose, you become sad.

Out of attachment, you believe that you possess. Attaching ourselves and depending are two such deeply rooted habits in us that they seem normal. On attaching yourself, fears arise, amongst which the main ones are: the fear of loss and the fear of rejection.

We pursue the object, the person, the pleasure or the substance that we depend on or are addicted to and our reasoning stops advising us appropriately. All this leads us in the end to a deep sadness. Sometimes it is so difficult to admit it and live with it that we surround ourselves with noise and outside stimuli or increase our dependence and addiction in order to 'cover over' or flee from this deep sadness. It is a dead-end street, a spiral that takes us down, and the consequences can be terrible.

To help ourselves get out of this pit, it is necessary to go far away from the atmosphere that has brought us to this state; we should have the desire to overcome it and accept outside help. Change direction, re-find your compass and leave the dark night to enter into the dawn. Dare to cross the threshold. You won't be alone. Trust.

Fear, anger and sadness originate in the habits of clinging, attaching oneself and depending. With them, our heart loses freedom. The pressure that these emotional states generate and the absence of true freedom cause us to suffer and even to feel ourselves to be victims or miserable.

We are so used to these forms of suffering that we come to believe that they are aspects of human nature and, therefore, natural. We are prepared to pay the price for staying dependent with stress, suffering and unhappiness to the point of getting ill. The natural state of the self is free and not being trapped by dependence. Sadness and suffering indicate to us that there is something unnatural and abnormal. It is possible to stop suffering these emotional upsets.

When you have a feeling of loss, you feel sad. Generally, this sadness about the situation precedes the feeling of hate, anger or frustration. If you observe your emotions closely, you can come to understand them.

Sometimes the sadness comes from a grief, for someone that has died, from a separation, from a brusque change that means a move from living one reality to another in a very short space of time. Living through the grief and overcoming it consists of making peace with the memories recorded on our memory. It is to reach a point that they do not upset us or cause us pain. It is to get to a point that this memory of what was and no longer is does not generate desires, dissatisfaction, frustration or sadness.

One does not get over the grief of a loved one, a lost child, a disappeared love, because one allows the memory to continue alive, in such a way that it invades awareness and colonizes the spirit. The images and the memories of experiences in the past come again and again onto the screen of the mind, bringing about different kinds of feelings that range from sadness to frustration. The memory suffocates the present, wanting to relive a past that can no longer exist. It ended.

The good news is that you choose what you are going to do and how you are going to respond. You choose what you think and what you feel. You have the possibility and the freedom to use your creative capacity to respond to the reality that surrounds you and to the stimuli that it throws at you at every moment. This means changing the predominant belief that the other—other people, society or the world—determines how you are and why you react as you do.

If you justify your responses by blaming the outside, you reduce your power to choose the answer. For example, if you say that you are sad each time it rains, then your sadness depends upon whether it rains or not; therefore, you give up your freedom to choose whether you get sad or not by depending on the weather.

In meditation you can contemplate your emotions and what goes through your mind. You will see and feel that emotions of fear and sadness arise, and, if you sit quietly with these emotions, you will be able to follow their tracks to the origin and you will see that you are clinging on to the belief that you can possess things and people. In the silence of your being this will also become senseless to you as you realize that you cannot possess anything or anyone. Not even your own body, since you are only inhabiting it.

As you go deeper into meditation, what used to be some real emotional tsunamis, which sucked out your energy, which is you, start abating gradually until they become gentle waves on the surface of consciousness. The time will come when even these little waves no longer appear. To reach this point you should meditate.

Frustration

The experience of frustration, besides being painful, is a driving force for growth.
Emilio Jorge Atognazza

Frustration arises out of a lack of emotional autonomy and unfulfilled expectations.

The woman loses hope because she does not achieve the opium of love. She gets frustrated. She does not find the emotionally mature man to share her life with. The man gets frustrated with the woman's emotional games and manipulation.

When frustration in a woman occurs because of professional matters, it often leads her to get close to a man motivated by his project, and she sticks herself to him. She lives out her dream through him. Your frustration as a woman also arises when you wash, clean, care for, attend to, run after, concern yourself with, shop, cook, pick up after, work outside and inside the home and feel that you are not on top of everything. Not only do they not recognize it or thank you for it, but on top of that they come to you with demands and complaints. It is frustrating.

On other occasions women feel unhappy and frustrated when they realize that men exploit them. They feel themselves to be victims. Their self-esteem is so low that they have accepted and continue to accept that behavior from them. But we cannot blame the man for this. It is the responsibility of both. The woman has to put limits, take care of herself and respect her space, to say 'no'. It is important to have the courage and bravery to establish limits in order to prevent abuse. While she has a need for dependence, she will not be able to find the inner power necessary to achieve it.

This is the co-dependence in which, in the relationship, each one consumes the other. It is a parasitical relationship. Between the victim, the oppressed person, and the oppressing person, the compassion usually goes towards the victim. The oppressor and the oppressed person are together for a reason. A symbiotic process is created between them both. There is no one who is an absolute victim nor an absolute abuser. The one collaborates with the other. Female neediness and toxic masculinity keep this intersection going.

As a result of this dynamic, some women become feminists out of this place of frustration. They condemn, they attack, denounce and discriminate. They end up considering the 'male race' a monster; it is a feminism invaded by toxic masculinity that uses the same resources, methods and tools. Like this we do not go forward. It produces opposite reactions from men and duality continues.

It is a feminism in which a woman flees from transforming herself from the inside out. It is a feminism that has not managed to propose a new paradigm with the collaboration and complicity of men. A commitment is required from everybody. But we will change little out of frustration.

To be the creator of changes you should adapt. This fact is very important in order to avoid getting frustrated and to continue enjoying each instant. During the day, it is possible that a great part of your energy is spent on fears, dependences, emotional reactions and frustration. You want to control the uncontrollable, you get frustrated, you want to control what the other does, know where he is, who with, etc. This thirst for control causes you anxiety, frustration and fear. You fear that things will not be or go as you want. The fears fix your attention on certain things, to the exclusion of others. Your vision and your world get smaller. You lose global perspective. You drown in a glass of water.

You have the freedom and the ability necessary to choose how you should respond to situations: you can accept, confront and change; or resist, fear, reject and flee. What you resist persists, and what you accept is transformed. The inflexibility that comes out of being stuck in frustration, in fear and/or resistance, blocks you and acts as a catalyst for the destruction of your own capacity to live fully, without blockages. If you get frustrated and complain, instead of facing a situation, you flee from it with fear. There is another option: you can stay serene and face the situation, understanding its meaning and freeing yourself from its impact. Flowing with it instead of succumbing to it.

Resignation

Women put up with things. They resign themselves. They do all they can to have a man a the pedestal and keep him tied to them. That way they act like martyrs and do not respect themselves. This dependence on their need turns into a dependent oppression.

Women 'lower' themselves, sometimes to maintain the

balance in the partnership. But if this makes them annul themselves and even accept mistreatment, they have chosen badly. Their relationship with him becomes suffocating.

In some environments, abuse has another meaning. For example, Marina Subirats explained to me how, in Bolivia, she talked to women in a market and one of them said to her: 'No, no, sometimes I tell my Pedrito to come and hit me in front of the others.' 'And why do you do that?' 'Well, if I don't, it means I don't matter to him any more. So, it's a way of showing that he loves me and that if I was talking to another man, this has made him jealous because he loves me and so he hits me. It is a way of reaffirming this love.' This happens as an agreed thing. It was the woman herself who said 'I call him so that all the other women see it because that way I show the others that I am still a loved woman.'

Women, to compensate and to keep themselves going, accept these mutilations. Their inability to respond to psychological or physical abuse arises out of the absence of respect for themselves. Through being submissive and dominated, they have no weapons to fight with. They feel clumsy, inept, incompetent, useless, unworthy and guilty. They need to get back their identity (see the section 'Female identities' in chapter 6) and to follow the steps to living in wholeness (see chapter 7).

Guilt

To grow means to accept guilt.
Joan Garriga

Guilt is useful if it doesn't lead you to self-destruction or unconsciously cause illnesses. Guilt allows us to recognize our mistakes, it allows for an exchange, a respect of the other. But if guilt is unhealthy, it blocks our creativity, it blocks our spontaneity and the chance to realize our dreams.
Guillermo Kozameh

To be able to take care of them, women need to identify with the other person, to have empathy and feel compassion. Women feel compassion for men in many moments. If something does not work, they blame themselves. Women feel guilty more easily than men do. They feel guilt for not having done what they should, for not having respected, for having rebelled. Men don't usually feel guilt so much; without guilt they feel more 'macho'.

If a marriage is going badly, the woman tends to think that it is her fault, because she has not respected this man enough, she hasn't carried out her duty sufficiently, given that she can't generate happiness, is incompetent, or has rebelled.

We have seen how the traditional woman needs to be a person through the man she loves. The man is the one who gives her a place in the world and she finds it logical to make herself pretty for him, speak for him, give herself to him, take care of him. If his eyes don't see her, she disappears; if he doesn't praise her dishes, she doesn't know how to cook; if he doesn't desire her sexually, it is because her sensuality and attractiveness have died; if he doesn't want to communicate with her, it is because she doesn't offer him anything of intelligence; if he doesn't love her, it is because she does not deserve it. And so, out of her submission and obedience to the man she has put on a pedestal, she feels incompetent and blames herself, harming herself and suffering uselessly.

On a night-time radio program that people ring for advice, I have heard women crying in desperation. They ring a lot because they are the victims of abuse, and almost always an element of guilt appears. They say: 'Well, perhaps I did something or perhaps I deserved it.' Sometimes they have reported their partner, they have even thrown them out of the house or have separated from them, or he has received an order to stay away from her. Then women feel sorry for them. The woman wants to go back, undo what she has done and withdraw the complaint or take the man in again. They themselves do not understand their guiltiness. They say: 'I don't know why I feel sorry for him.' 'But listen,' the radio presenter answers them, 'didn't he abuse you? This man is an abuser, but how can you accept that he treats you like that? You even had to go to the hospital; he left you injured! How can you accept it?' He takes their guilt away from them and they keep on insisting: 'I feel bad and so I want to withdraw the complaint because if I don't I won't be able to feel alright.'

Many of us as women still feel that we are transgressing the norms by not accepting the law that tradition imposes. As transgressors, we will have 'a punishment', which might be being alone or a frequent phantom: the loss of affection. You are invaded by the anguish of thinking that you have done something that is a transgression and, therefore, you are going to get the punishment that you deserve. The essence of guilt is moral self-reproach: I did something bad when I could have done something else.

Perhaps it was you who broke up the relationship and he is destroyed. Perhaps you had an affair and now you feel bad. Perhaps you have children and you are afraid they will feel unhappy. Guilt hides criticism and generates self-punishment. You feel bad and on top of that you punish yourself, so that you allow yourself to be trapped by a spiral of blame and punishment that blows the situation up into tragic proportions.

Guilt does not allow for correction; it only leaves room for punishment. Sometimes we can fall into the trap of compensation. Guilt can push us towards the past, to try to please the people we feel guilty about.

Guilt implies choice and responsibility, whether you are aware of it or not. You should be clear about what is and what isn't in your hands. What is or isn't a transgression or a rupture of your integrity. Without this understanding you might come to take on guilt in a totally inappropriate way.

Are you creative when it comes to punishing yourself? Change the focus and learn to be creative in order to be loving with yourself out of acceptance and understanding.

Why do we punish ourselves? Perhaps we don't feel that we deserve something: 'I don't have the right to…' If others see that you treat yourself like that, they will also treat you in that way. How will they value you if you don't value yourself? You fail, you fall down, you make mistakes and you feel unworthy. You take your errors too much to heart.

You see yourself according to how others value you, and, if you don't manage to fulfill their expectations, you punish yourself by feeling guilty about it.

Let's be honest: sometimes we would rather feel guilty than change. The guilt whereby we do not take on the responsibility of changing leads us to punish ourselves. We prefer to punish ourselves rather than change a pattern of behavior. With this attitude, we feel heavy and burdened. We are rigid, we find it hard to flow and adapt. Emotional intelligence teaches us that we achieve nothing by allocating guilt, since that turns us into helpless victims. Let us accept responsibility. It will be difficult as long as there is a psychological, emotional and/or physical dependence.

An act of integrity can put straight the guilt that arises out of having harmed your integrity. When you free yourself of guilt, you live in peace inside yourself. You accept responsibility and stop martyring yourself. Accepting responsibility is constructive; it allows all your potential to stay awake. Feeling free and unburdened means to heal the heart so as not to take on the guilt, bitterness or hate for things that have already happened and that you can't change. It means learning to accept, forgive, forget and let go.

Guilt advises you that there is something you should put right. If you are prepared to see it, to enter into dialogue and clear it up, you are on the right path. Becoming aware is good; it is the base of any positive change. The important thing is not to be a martyr. Learn the lesson. Say sorry, if it is necessary. Rectify. To do so, it helps to go within, observe, see and understand.

With the practice of meditation you will be able to make the changes you want to, or the old patterns of behavior will diminish the effectiveness of your efforts, like the tide that washes away the sandcastle on the beach.

When you connect to the authenticity of what you really are, you re-find your serenity: you put a stop to the repetitive thoughts that make you unhappy. You realize that, when you project onto others and blame them for your anger, believing that they have hurt you, you allow yourself to be their slave and victim. Bill Clinton telephoned Nelson Mandela two hours after he left prison, after many years of imprisonment for having worked to disseminate human rights, and he asked him how he could forgive them so easily. Mandela answered that, if he were to hate them, they would continue to control him.

Hate

Hate is one of the three hellish states, according to Buddhism. The other two are dependence and indifference.

You hate because the other hasn't acted as you would have liked. That your expectations haven't been met or that the other hasn't fulfilled what they seemed to promise causes hate, anger, fury and rage.

In fact, if you hate someone, look at yourself: the hate is towards yourself and towards the universe. You are angry with the world. The universe is not dancing according to your desires.

If the man breaks up the relationship, it is a betrayal, and the woman feels that he should pay for it. To get rid of that figure, she has to deny it. If she doesn't hate him, she cannot go on living. So she criticizes him, she speaks badly of him. She needs to find his faults in order to free herself from him. 'Since you have destroyed me, to survive I have to destroy you.' Blackmail ploys are used so that the other might understand and feel the pain that one feels oneself. You want to punish the other because they haven't been as you wanted them to be. There is no compassion, rather punishment.

You hate justifying yourself in the other. You expected a lot from him and he has let you down. He has hurt you and broken your heart. You respond to this wound with revenge. You have to make him pay for it. You think that way justice will be done. That anger keeps you tied to the being that you hate. Instead of letting them go and forgiving them, you bind yourself to them even tighter, feeding the pain and conflict.

Hate is an 'incendiary' emotion; it destroys the concentration and kills our capacity to act with dignity and excellence.

You cannot love one and hate another. A heart that contains hate will have a contaminated love.

Can hate justify things? Can it make things better? Can hating be healthy from any point of view?

Hate affects your health, it 'poisons' your heart, it kills your inner peace, it dries out your love and happiness and you remain isolated in your loneliness that is darkened by that rage. Take a moment to reflect on the last time that you hated someone. It might be difficult to see that your anger is not created by anyone except yourself. Although it 'seems' that the way the other person acted is responsible for your emotional state, the truth is that hate is your response. Each response that you give can be a conscious choice. You forget that you have the possibility of choosing because it seems that the hatred arises naturally from inside you. In reality, you are allowing yourself to act on automatic pilot: your subconscious habits based on your beliefs and your perception make up your conscious thoughts and actions. It is the sign of mental and emotional laziness. In that state, your intelligence 'sleeps' and it is impossible to think clearly and take precise decisions.

To free yourself from this habit, you need to take four important steps:

Understand that hate is not healthy. When you have a feeling of loss, you feel sad. This sadness about the situation generally precedes the feeling of hate, anger or frustration. Understand your emotions by observing them closely.

Accept that you are responsible for your own anger.

The other is free to act as they like; you cannot change them. But you can improve on your response.

Be prepared to observe, challenge and change the beliefs and perceptions that you base yourself on and that are rooted in your emotional pain. Some of these beliefs make your anger stronger and block your learning. For example, when you think that it is alright that you are angry, that to feel anger is the natural and normal reaction in the face of certain situations. Another belief is that anger causes your adrenaline to flow and you think it is a healthy addiction that makes you feel 'alive', that having sudden rushes of adrenaline makes you feel energetic and strong. And you use any pretext—for example, the double-parked car that has not let you pass—to feel bad, and, thanks to the car in front, your adrenaline level has risen!

Emotional suffering is an indication that you have to change something in yourself, but what happens when you don't change anything? You ignore the messenger, and the stress you suffer from continues to grow. Finally it turns into such a habit that, if you relax, 'de-stress yourself', you feel uncomfortable! You have got used to your stress.

Become aware of the need to evaluate your beliefs and the repercussions that they have in your life. That way you will be more prepared to change and improve your habits. This is the first step that you should take to achieve it.

'It is impossible to get angry and laugh at the same time,' Wayne W. Dyer reminds us.[6] Anger and laughter are mutually exclusive and you have enough power to choose either of the two. Each time you choose to get angry because of another's behavior, you are depriving them of their right to be what they choose.

You are capable of forgiving, and finally, forgetting, in order to go on with your life without carrying for any longer the pain that makes you live in the past and does not allow you to enjoy the present. This is the base from which to re-establish the power of your heart and your capacity to love. Direct your attention within; detach yourself from all your thoughts, feelings, habits and memories. This will allow you to get closer to the heart of your conscience, to the center of your being. Thus will you find your natural state of peace, your way of loving, and happiness will well up in you. You will re-find your true heart intact, your spiritual heart, capable of embracing without bitterness, capable of loving without putting limiting conditions.

Loneliness

There is no doubt that loneliness is painful, but so is the betrayal of oneself, and each person, on their own, in the said dilemmas, has to decide what price they are willing to pay.
Pilar Jericó[7]

Due to the lack of true encounter between men and women, loneliness is an experience of more and more people. Men hide behind a frenetic activity that keeps them busy and far from their heart. Women have copied this path.

Sometimes the loneliness occurs when the other abandons you. The experience of Marina, a woman abandoned by her husband, is explained to us by Mar Correa:[8] 'You feel the unpopulated hollow of your heart, the deep well of the empty cupboard, the solitary echo of silence, the empty side of the bed, the uninhabited nights, the freezing weather that invades the corners of your being.'

Although thanks to the Internet it is easy to meet people and establish relationships with them, those relationships quickly unravel when we don't find the satisfaction that we had imagined. The feeling of loneliness that we were trying to avoid increases.

In liquid, ephemeral, passing relationships, one ends up being afraid of being used and discarded. So you protect yourself behind walls of privacy and try to let nothing, not even love, alter you or make you feel strange. Relationships are toyed with in a superficial game in which the true beings are hidden. The character tells its story, the external face dominates. The being remains alone. You don't dare to express yourself as you are. Your character expresses itself, not you.

Sometimes we have the impulse to be submissive, abandoning our own personality with the aim of overcoming the feeling of loneliness and impotence. It is as if we renounced the self and submerged ourselves in the outside world. We become extrovert and don't take care of our personal development. We lose touch with the essential. We say that the external is responsible for how we feel. We have given up our power to the outside and we live from the outside in and not the inside out. That is, we allow the outside to determine how we are and feel.

Something happens to Anna that many women could identify with. Anna is afraid of loneliness. She always tries to please and be nice. So as not to risk rejection, she always agrees with others. That way she feels accepted and part of the group. She renounces being herself out of fear of being alone. She gives up her power to others and turns into a puppet who allows others to mold her according to what they want from her. She lives 'from the outside in', that is, the outside determines how she is on the inside. Sometimes the price to pay for not allowing oneself the risk of being different and being yourself is very high.

Out of the fear of loneliness, we flee from it. We hide it with the daily routine of activities, the security and approval that we find in private and social relationships, success at work and in business, or in any other form that means a distraction in the end. But whistling in the darkness does not attract light. The loneliness, fear and anxiety remain. Then the person, insecure of themselves, cannot bear the burden that freedom imposes on them; they have to flee from it by seeking escape mechanisms, if they do not manage to progress from negative freedom to the positive (being responsible for their own decision and acts). The main collective forms of evasion in our time are represented by the submission to a leader, a guru, football, sensual pleasures, excessive consumption. The individual forms of evasion would be those that one depends on and that make one addicted to gambling, to sex, to drugs or alcohol, amongst other objects of addiction.

Sometimes, the state of loneliness, insecurity and power-lessness, when an inner void is created, when creativity is 'atrophied' and the emotions are blocked, is unbearable. To get over it, you have two options: overcome this situation or succumb to it. With the first, you are able to go towards 'positive freedom', whereby you accept your personal rule and can establish your connection with the world in love and work spontaneously, in the genuine expression of your emotional, sensitive and intellectual faculties: in this way, you will join humanity, nature and yourself again, without stripping yourself of the integrity and independence of your individual and unique self.

With the other option you go backwards: you abandon your freedom and try to overcome the loneliness by eliminating the gap that has opened up between your individual personality and the group (family, collective or the world), generating dependences, addictions and a considerable mental and emotional imbalance.

If a person isn't mentally stable, they don't have enough emotional strength, lack balance and have not nourished themselves spiritually; even if they have all this range of possible freedoms, they feel alone, insecure and with inner deficiencies. They often try to fill that void through consumption, not only of products, objects and properties, but also of creativity from the outside in. When you go to see a film, you consume the creativity of other people, you are a consumer, not a creator; the same thing occurs when you watch the television. I am not saying it is a bad thing to see films. Simply, one should be careful not to avoid oneself through escaping the self.

The problem is not so much of physical loneliness, but of moral loneliness. You can be alone in the physical sense but have a spiritually rich inner world and be relating to ideas, values or, at least, social norms that provide a feeling of communion and belonging. On the other hand, you can live amongst people and allow yourself to be overcome by a feeling of total isolation: disconnected from values, symbols or norms, incapable of communicating and feeling weak, anxious and powerless.

Being with people is not necessarily what helps us to get over the feeling of loneliness. The greater the connection based on values (love, brotherhood, complicity, empathy, solidarity, etc.) and on spiritual contents that give meaning to the relationship, the more one feels that they belong to the human family and global community. Isolation is *maya;*[9] it is a mental mirage, since everything is interconnected and as human beings we form part of this local and global interconnection.

These days, especially in western societies, we have many resources, facilities and means. What is more, human relationships have been made freer: you can be married, divorced, get married again, live together, be with two people, or three, or alone. A great range of options and possibilities exist that, not long ago, were difficult to imagine.

We see that, in spite of the great freedom that — as individuals, as human beings and as a collective — we have achieved, even so, the experience of fear, pain and loneliness has increased. We haven't known how to use freedom to strengthen ourselves emotionally, mentally and spiritually. Out of the fear of experiencing more pain, we close our heart and remain blocked and alone.

If you don't expect anything of anyone, you will not have the fears connected to expectations. If others share with you, fine, and, if not, also fine. That greed of wanting attention, wanting respect, wanting love, leaves us in a state of permanent emptiness. No human being can satisfy our deepest hungers. They might be able to help us in some situations, but, at bottom, the reality is that we are alone.

All people should be alone from time to time, to establish an inner dialogue and discover their personal strength. In aloneness you understand that harmony and peace of the spirit can only be found in yourself, and not from others. Wherever you go, you go with yourself. If you are fine with yourself, it will be easier to feel fine in your surroundings and with others. If you feel comfortable, you won't flee from yourself or from aloneness. You will enjoy being alone and being with others.

Cultivate your creativity in order to build and improve the relationship between the feminine and the masculine that there is in you. Sometimes you spend the time wishing that 'another' would satisfy and fill the space of the deficiencies that you feel. But you will fill that emptiness when you connect again to your true essence.

Sustaining a good relationship with yourself means to relate to your being, to be in harmony with your mind, with your emotions, with your spirit and with your body. If you do not sustain a good emotional relationship with yourself, then you abuse the body by generating addictions.

Liquid relationships

We love on our own terms, making love into a commercial thing. We have a mercantile mentality and love is not for sale, it is not a question of monetary exchange. It is a state of being in which all human problems are resolved.
Krishnamurti[10]

We live at a time when the consumer society has created the rule of the sell-by date. This has been transferred to relationships. Not only do products become out of date, so do relationships. The points of reference of our security have gone and we are invaded by uncertainty. We are afraid of making lasting relationships. Our bonds are fragile and seem only to depend on the profits they generate.

They are ephemeral relationships, without commitment. They satisfy certain needs at specific times. They are relationships of a mutual lack of knowing, of the other and of oneself. You end up going to bed with someone for the sake of an orgasm, a momentary pleasure, ephemeral. It has generated an addiction to pleasure.

When relationships cover needs that generate dependence and addiction, they become unhealthy; they are impulsive and passionate. These uncontrolled desires end up harming the relationship and the people involved in it.

'We stay in relationship to someone only while that relationship gratifies us, provides us with shelter, satisfies us. But the moment that relationship is upset by something that makes us uncomfortable, we discard it. In other words, the relationship exists as long as we feel gratified.'[11]

Men and women are desperate to relate, as they feel easily 'discardable' and abandoned to managing with their own resources. We are hungry to find the security that union offers us. Hungry to find someone to lean on in difficult moments. Hungry to relate to someone in order to escape from ourselves and the isolation towards which aloneness can push us. At the same time, we do not trust that the relationship might last forever. The fear exists that this might turn into an unbearable burden, into a cage that may limit our freedom. Thus, the idea of relationship is laden with attraction and threat at the same time. It attracts because of the pleasure of the possible union. It threatens to be a trap that encloses us and suffocates us. That is why we hear more and more talk of connecting and less of relating. We want to be connected, in a network.

Liquid loves of the present have a point of pain: the art of breaking up relationships is easier than the art of making and building them. We are not prepared to take on a lasting commitment. It is curious to see in the statistics that during holiday periods a greater number of marriage break-ups are registered. It is during those periods when the couple could find time for quietness, serenity, sharing, taking decisions calmly.

There is a space for shared living and closeness. Yet it is precisely then when an explosion occurs.

The effort to perpetuate shared living and to conserve the relationship of the new couple lies on the one hand in maintaining emotional and sexual honesty, and, on the other, requires a purpose that goes beyond oneself and the relationship, a shared project. Transcending oneself and living out the spiritual dimension brings meaning and wholeness to the relationship. Couples break up because the excitement dissolves like a lump of sugar. Daily life is dominated by rushing around, work obligations, domestic chores, childcare responsibilities, the demands and the reproaches, the complaints and the blaming, economic and health problems, stress, lack of communication... and all of this spills out like an acid that corrodes the love and foundations of the relationship. There are more and more people who live without committing themselves and without being in love. Zygmunt Bauman, in his book *Liquid Love*, explains:

A successful little short-lived relationship is pleasant and brief. We can suppose that it is pleasant because it is brief. It is pleasant precisely because one is aware that one doesn't have to make much effort, thus feeling that way for longer. In fact, one doesn't have to do anything in order to enjoy it. A short-lived relationship is the incarnation of what is instant and disposable. But the relationship won't have these qualities if certain conditions are not fulfilled. First condition, you have to go into the relationship with total awareness and clarity, no falling in love, no emotion that might bind it or upset it is allowed. Second condition: keep things in this state and do not occupy other terrain, keep it contained and controlled.

In these times of instability in relation to love, women's level of sacrifice has reduced. They themselves have placed the limits. They don't want to suffer any more or submit to the other's power. Which means that more and more women are living alone. According to Correa,[12] in 2006, 35% of the Spanish population aged between 25 and 40 were living alone and most of them were women, not only because the number of separations has increased by 60% in the last decade, but because as women we have learned to discover a fundamental space of our own where we can develop as individuals. We no longer need the male presence at our side to feel useful, busy, fed or protected. We know how to give ourselves recognition without needing it through a man's eyes.

Other interesting data brought to us by the Spanish National Institute of Statistics are the following: from 1991 to 2001, the number of people who started to live alone increased by 81.9%. Specifically, the number of young single people aged between 25 and 34 who live alone increased by 208.7%.[13] In Catalonia, a specific survey of homes was carried out in 2007, when 541,769 single households were detected (out of a total of 2,782,300).[14]

With all we have seen over these past pages, it is clear that couples today are dealing with a society in crisis. A restructuring that allows for the new requirements is urgent. It is important to work together for a change in attitude amongst men, starting with the education they receive at home and at school, so that they do not continue to try to act like the privileged male in the face of women, marriage, children, sex and work. We also have to work together for a change in women's attitude, so that they stop emotionally manipulating and feeling themselves to be victims. If we don't achieve these changes, living together will continue to fall apart, divorce rates will continue to rise, and the family unit will continue to fluctuate. We will remain in a state of continuous dissatisfaction.

Permanent dissatisfaction

Not getting what you want is sometimes a great stroke of luck.
Dalai Lama

The consumer society has created a culture of accumulation and materialism that, however much we have, does not satisfy us. It is an illusion that generates an apparent satisfaction inside us. But when you look into the mirror of your heart you find sadness, suffering and emptiness. Dissatisfaction.

We are living in moments of uncertainty. Insecurity often seizes us. We have a lot, of everything. We can choose. Even so, dissatisfaction seems to be a constant.

We live with different and sometimes contradictory models. We want to leave behind the dominant patriarchy, masculine toxicity, and free ourselves of dependent and submissive femininity. But they have invaded our external and internal system to the point that a true change of consciousness is necessary if we want to be able to free ourselves of it. We have gone in a few decades from upholding relationships of commitment and responsibility to others of desire and pleasure. Relationships have gone from being to having, so that now you have it and then you change it for another. There is little will when it comes to working to keep up a relationship. If it doesn't work for me, I leave it and change it for another. We don't face things. We flee. We separate. This, in some way, perpetuates the dissatisfaction.

What perpetuates this dissatisfaction in both women and men?

Let us see some causes.

Maintaining patterns

If we don't change our way of satisfying a need arising out of the mirage I mentioned before, we perpetuate the dissatisfaction. The dissatisfaction is perpetuated by:

- Always maintaining the same pattern of relationships
- Not realizing that, although you change a person and relationship, the pattern is maintained
- Change takes place on the outside, but inwardly the same addictions, behavior and attitudes are maintained

Woman tries to meet her needs by following the models sold by advertising images, which, in sum, perpetuate dependent neediness. We do things that are not natural. We focus on cultivating an image and disconnect from our being.

Erin Pizzey founded a house in London for abused women. After twenty-five years of experience she published a book, *Prone to Violence*, in which she speaks of a reality that she experienced during those years: of the abused women that she took in, an average of up to 90%, on leaving the shelter, returned to similar situations or the same men. They hit them physically but the women returned to them. They were addicted to violence.

Addictions make us keep on with the same pattern of behavior. The brain and its addictions rule and awareness has given over its power to habit. Joe Dispensa explains to us: 'The main reason why most people cannot use their capacity to change is that they have become too addicted to their feelings and bodily emotions.'[15]

Laziness also makes us continue functioning according to our old personality. When you are influenced by laziness, you stop being alert and make excuses. A lack of care prevails. And so a lot of energy is wasted on disorganization, lack of precision, errors, etc., and you perpetuate the dissatisfaction.

Attention is fundamental if we want to change patterns and overcome addictions and laziness.

Beliefs

Our beliefs limit us, our past conditions us and our fears prevent us from living out our deepest dreams. We live in accordance to a series of beliefs that make up our view of life, our attitudes, decisions and behavior.

These beliefs are cultural, political, religious and/or spiritual. They are beliefs about what is good and what is bad; about what is success and what is failure. And an endless list of beliefs that make up 'the box' in which we live.

We believe that the need will be satisfied with such a man or such a woman. This is perpetuated by society, advertising, culture and tradition. It is a false belief generated by stereotypes that lead us to an incessant battle to achieve something that is almost impossible.

Our other half is inside, not outside. You are a 'whole', with no need to depend on the other. You are complete. The other can complement you. Complementarity is possible when you are both complete 'spheres'. Get your personal sovereignty back and that way you will feel whole. This state capacitates you to love without depending, love and be free, love without fear preventing it. To do all this you have to revise your beliefs. Do you think that to love you need to worry obsessively? Do you think that worries are healthy, bring you health, well-being, help you to channel the energy of your mind, and allow you to find solutions? If the answer is 'No', look again at why you keep worrying.

By keeping your worries you are not making good use of your life energy. One of a person's main energies is the energy of thought.

There are mental dependences that arise out of a badly channeled imagination, false beliefs or mental weakness. For example, this happens when the pattern of repetitive thoughts makes you wallow in feelings of guilt. Or you think, almost obsessively, that someone wishes you harm or is after you. You create realities based on non-proven suppositions. They are negative and self-destructive mental habits. You fall into repetitive thoughts, which lead you to be constantly unhappy.

Find out what thoughts are behind the feelings of unhappiness or pressure that you feel: 'Maybe I won't arrive on time', 'If I don't hand it in on time, I will lose the job', 'If I don't do this, they will stop appreciating me'. In these kinds of thoughts there is the fear of losing something if you don't manage to meet some expectations. This fear exercises a pressure that lessens your ability to achieve your aims. For this not to happen, change the course of the thoughts that you are having. Have ideas and memories of trust and enthusiasm instead of ideas and memories weighed down by insecurity and fears. To do so you should detect those beliefs that have an influence on the creation of your thoughts. There are thoughts determined by your belief about what success and failure are, what it is to win and what to lose. There are beliefs that, although we accept them, are not true; they are like a veil that prevent us from seeing clearly, and that generate in us thoughts of fear and feelings of pressure.

Stopping, observing, reinterpreting, re-evaluating, controlling thoughts and feelings and changing beliefs requires energy. Not an energy that you will get from the outside, rather the true energy that you have within. The power of truth, of authenticity, provides us with the energy to change. The truth is deeper than beliefs. In fact, many beliefs are false and that is why they cause us states of anxiety and suffering when we allow them to influence our perception of reality.[16]

We are the creators of our realities. Reality in itself does not cause us stress, pain or unhappiness. It is our perception and interpretation of reality that causes these reactions. Revise how you perceive situations and with what beliefs you interpret and judge them.

Reinterpreting the situation, the concrete reality, means to allow the old perception to die in order to make room for a new vision. If the old doesn't die, the new cannot be built correctly.

Fear of rejection

The fear of rejection keeps us dependent. There is a saying: 'Hell hath no fury like a woman scorned.' For a man it is also very painful to feel rejected or abandoned by a woman, especially if he has made a commitment and formed a family with her.

From the fear of rejection comes the fear of being different or of being perceived as someone different. You should be careful of what you are afraid of, because you invoke it. Fear is like a magnet. If you are afraid of something happening to you, and even visualize it happening to you, this terrorizes you; it terrifies you and shuts you into a state of fear. What you are doing is invoking this to happen, because the power of the mind and visualization is very strong. If you are afraid you will be robbed, afraid of falling over, afraid of losing, you are invoking the theft, the fall, the loss.

Fear of rejection produces rejection.

In our present-day society we are suffering from an increase in violence. It is an increase in arbitrary violence, not only the organized kind. By arbitrary violence I mean that it seems sudden and not planned. In random shootings, groups of young people who alone would not attack anybody, as soon as they are in a group, something arises in their mass consciousness, in the group, and their behavior becomes arbitrarily violent.

Perhaps at the peak of this is insecurity, a fear of rejection or of ending up alone. A need exists to connect to others. We have the need to belong to a group and we are afraid of them rejecting us. This is more marked in young people. They look for the approval of the rest and it is frowned upon to stand out or be different. This fear turns us into submissive people, dependent and addicted.

Who are most likely to be slaves to the fear of rejection? Those who most need to belong to a group. That is, those who have most need of affiliation or those who take refuge in the group to escape from loneliness.

The fear of rejection is painful and addictive at the same time. Rejection hurts and generates anger and the desire for revenge. The person doing the rejecting will find it difficult to separate emotionally from the life of the one who has been rejected.

Socially, rejection generates violence. The fear of rejection works in such a way that you amplify the experience of the rejection and you generate anger against yourself or against others. The corresponding attitude to attack is the aggressive one. Aggressiveness takes on many forms. For example, rudeness or abuse. The ultimate origin of violent behavior is that the soul was not nurtured as it needed to be: loved, cared for, respected, valued. Now it has to make a great effort to be able to maintain a balanced and healthy mind and to strengthen its bases in order to construct a solid and lasting self-esteem.

When we feel rejected and we take it as proof of our imperfections, it is difficult for us to risk showing ourselves as we are again. We put on armor to protect ourselves from the shame, the anger, the depression and anxiety that rejection causes us.

Rejection can lead us to the shame that we may have felt in our childhood. If you start to feed ideas such as that you are boring or undesirable, it is possible that you will end up avoiding intimacy and never allow anyone to know you. Or that you go on to the defensive and reject people because you fear that, when they see what you are really like, they will think you are not worth it. The fear of rejection intensifies when you think you are inferior to others.

If you recognize that rejection is not a condemnation, but rather an experience that we all have to deal with again and again, it will be easier for you to bear and overcome. You continue to be valuable, independently of the approval or disapproval of others.

Not saying 'no'

Not being able to say 'no', because of our insecurities, keeps us dependent. We do not value ourselves or we value the other and their priorities more. We put the feelings, needs and desires of other people first. We sacrifice ourselves for the other. The question is: what are you afraid of losing that prevents you from saying 'no' when you want to? Perhaps you haven't placed the limits for your personal space: mental, emotional, physical and spiritual. When they are transgressed, it is possible that you easily forget that you have the right to count on that space. Not only do you allow others to transgress it, but sometimes it is as if you put up a sign saying: 'Welcome, intruders'. This attracts harmful relationships, people whose scheme for survival consists in abuse, be it in a subtle or extreme form. Not establishing limits and welcoming intruders turns into a strategy that allows you to get their attention, approval and affection. Thus do poor versions of love appear. Thus do we continue to be needy and dependent.

When you find yourself faced with diverse situations, directions, proposals and opportunities, which of them do you say 'yes' to and which 'no'?

To make up your mind, it is very important to stay clear about the vision of your dream, your longings, what your soul really wants. You should be aware of what is essential for you. From this space of inner clarity, you should see which of these situations/opportunities go in the direction of your dream and the essential, and which distance you; which are like 'mirages', seeming to offer something easy and desirable, but will in truth distance you from the essential. They are opportunities that seem easier and, out of laziness, it would be more comfortable to say 'yes'. But inside you, if you listen, you know that, in the long or short term, you won't be happy, given that you avoid (or flee from) challenge. You haven't listened to your heart. You have allowed yourself to be carried away by inertia. Gandhi wrote: 'We should refuse to allow ourselves to be carried away by the current. A drowning human being cannot save others.'

Saying 'no' assertively and with positive energy means that you have reflected on it, that you have good reasons for saying 'no', and they are not against anybody or anything. That is, your 'no' arises out of a positive energy and not from the fear of rejection or bitterness. You recognize that there is something to do; you feel empathy towards the person or situation and you value it. But you explain to the other person that for you now, it is not the moment. You do not need to tell a compassionate lie; you can speak with honesty. With empathy, you manage to get the other person to take on board that, on this occasion, it is not you that has to do what is needed. You offer alternatives, creative ideas or solutions, showing your care and attention.

In this sense, the 'no' is a positive 'no' that arises out of a space of love, courage and respect. It is to say 'yes' to saying 'no'.

Giving up your power

On looking for the reference points of your being on the outside, you automatically distance yourself from your own center, your nucleus of strength. You give power to others to determine how you are, what you do and how you do it. Disconnected from your nucleus of inner power, you will never be satisfied with yourself or the other.

Pay attention to the situations in which you allow the other to impress you. Feeling impressed is not bad, but you can fall into the temptation of staying trapped in the superfluous and in appearances. What impresses you influences and even molds your awareness in that moment. You lose the ability to create your thoughts and feelings and these are influenced by the impression that you have allowed the other person to leave in you. Sometimes the impression is so large that you abandon yourself to it. You give up your power to the other, and let them dominate your emotional world. Nathaniel Branden, in his book *The Six Pillars of Self-Esteem*, explains his experience of allowing himself to be impressed and feel admiration towards another human being: 'On occasions, the temptation to betray oneself can be worse with those people that most interest us. I learned that no amount of admiration towards another human being can justify the sacrifice of one's own criteria.'

The consequences involved in allowing oneself to be impressed are various and occur on different levels. For example, when you are impressed by the position of the other—the boss, the mayor, the president, the top of the tops (and it is usually male because perhaps in a woman it would not impress us so much... I leave *that* as a subject open for reflection)—it is alright to respect their authority and their position. But when you allow their position to impress you, your ability to relate fluidly with that person is blocked. This can hinder your authority over your own life and open communication.

Another example is the situation whereby you are impressed by the other's achievements. You put them on a pedestal. You compare yourself with him or her. You have weak feelings about yourself, such as that you are not as good or effective as them, or you feel jealousy or guilt. All this is an obstacle on your path towards your own goals. Instead of being happy for the other's achievement, you feel small or you envy them. That way we do not support each other, we do not build together. We continue competing.

When you are impressed by the other's communication skills, you repress yourself and do not show the best of yourself. You become more clumsy than you really are. Out of admiration you can value, observe and enrich yourself, learning from the qualities and talent of the other.

It is good to recognize and appreciate the achievements and skills of others. But when you allow them to impress you, in some way you submit yourself to their influence and weaken your self-esteem and respect towards yourself. Without realizing it, you use the other to fill a gap or a lack that you feel in yourself. This will not always work. It will not strengthen you; it will rather generate a dependence that will weaken you.

In order to feel yourself and live in wholeness you should have mastery over your inner world. If it is not thus, you will only be able to feel temporary moments of wholeness. Besides, to attain wholeness you not only have to have inner sovereignty but also to check whether there is any crack or door left open to weakness in your personality. If you strengthen yourself on the one hand and on the other you are weakened, you will never reach that state of inner power.

If on the one hand you fill a bucket with water but it has holes or cracks, for all the water you pour into the bucket, it will continue emptying itself. The same can happen to you. That is why you have to discover the holes and cracks of your personality through which there are leaks of energy, where the responsibility lies for the fact that your efforts do not yield the results that you hope for. However much you try to fill it, the void generated by these losses continues.

Getting back your inner power means to recognize that you need to have a greater mastery over your inner world and your resources and faculties, such as the mind, the intellect, characteristics, conditioning and the habits of your personality.

Recognize that you should strengthen values such as tolerance, acceptance and flexibility if you want to survive the times of turbulence and changes that we are living in peacefully. Be aware that you are the one responsible for your present state.

Any weakness, inconsistency, dispersion, lack of focus and inner fluctuation will rob you of the energy necessary to feel whole. You should take positive risks in order to give yourself that power. Free yourself of any aspect that overshadows you. Allow your being to manifest itself and express itself with all its light.

We do not let go: together in revenge

After a divorce, often the woman seeks revenge against the man. The same thing happens the other way round when the man mistreats the woman as a way of revenge. That way anger takes control of the person. This keeps them in a loop of dependence. They have gone from a loving dependence to a bitter dependence. That way the woman's desire for power and authority over the other takes control of her, of her wish to punish him and make him suffer, which keeps him tied to her. She wants to sabotage him in everything. It is a twisted energy that she uses to punish the man.

In the main, men in general find it difficult to become aware of this emotional blackmail. That is why they struggle to understand these twisted games of women. In the history of ancient Greece we find many examples of this emotional blackmail.

For example, we have the story of Medea, who out of jealousy and revenge killed the two sons she had with her husband, since he had fallen in love with another woman thanks to which he could be a prince.

Another story of woman's manipulation (in Greece) is the one organized by the mother of Nero, Julia Agrippina, who had desires for power and so manipulated things in such a way that in the end her son organized a murder attempt against her.

Let us look at other aspects that keep dissatisfaction in play.

Desire is given more weight than commitment

Today desire is given more importance than commitment. After so many years of repressing desires, of feeling as if they were a sin, now we have gone to the other extreme.

Desires dominate us. We are ruled by our drives. We are like the shipwrecked at the mercy of desires that carry us like the waves, the winds and the currents, from one side to another with no clear destination. We lose the steering wheel of our life.

To reach a balance between desire and commitment, emotion and reason, passion and serenity, a great inner work is necessary, and, above all, having vision: What and where do I want to reach, what do I want to keep, what am I prepared to let go of or give up, in order to reach where I want to go?

Narcissism

Narcissistic individualism neither satisfies nor offers wholeness. Running from or rejecting the other, we do not achieve wholeness. Individualism, driven mainly from the United States, has brought achievements with it, such as a great personal freedom and independence, but it has atrophied us emotionally, especially when the I comes before the we, and we lose the skill of living together, communicating, listening and being in dialogue. We neither practice tolerance nor share healthily. On being with the other, or others, we lose inner peace and so we opt for narcissistic aloneness. This reduces the possibility of developing qualities and inner powers that are necessary in shared living, such as co-operation, asking, offering and agreeing; dialogue; active listening; empathy; loving and allowing oneself to be loved; confronting: letting go, forgiving and a long etcetera.

Let us remember the words of Farid Uddin Attar: 'If you destroy your self during one single day, you will be shining even though you are in darkness all the night. Don't say the word I, you who have, because of the I, fallen into a hundred disgraces' (*El lenguaje de los pájaros* [The Language of Birds]).

Other aspects which perpetuate the emptiness and dissatisfaction

- Feeling that you don't deserve any better.
- Comparing yourself. You believe the other is better than you. You are always the one who has to improve because you are worse. You make mistakes and you don't deserve more. You become smaller.
- Trying to be perfect. Feeling pressured by the perfection that you pursue and never reach.
- Not respecting yourself. This means not respecting your needs, your spaces, your limits.
- When you are not 'inspired' you feel bored and dissatisfied. As Anthony Robbins says: 'There are no lazy people, only people with impotent aims: that is, objectives that do not provide them with inspiration.'
- You don't know your true identity and you feel disappointed because possibly you haven't listened to or asked some in-depth questions, such as:
  —who are you?
  —what do you want in life?
  —what are your priorities?
  —what is your true dream, the most intimate in you?
  —where do you want to go? Where would you like to arrive?

With your being rooted in yourself, in who you are, you do not allow yourself to be led by impulses nor by sudden reactions. You keep your vision fixed on what you want and you know how to prioritize. You go forward surely and with certainty.

Understanding the erroneous mechanisms we use to fill our emptiness

Anger

Using violence, we will not find a harmonious sustainable solution. In anger and bitterness we remain in our deficiencies. With rage, we project ourselves outwards and the solution does not come because the change has to begin in you (I have dealt with a related theme in the section 'Hate' above).

For example, imagine that one day you get angry with William for something he has said or done. When anger is provoked in you, you create a register, an impression, a trace on your memory with the emotion of the anger. On that register is included the image of William mixed up with the emotion of anger. Three days later, walking down the street, you see a familiar person walking towards you in the opposite direction. That image enters your awareness and fits with that of William, whom you have already registered. So the thought pops up: 'That's William', accompanied by the emotion of anger. The anger enters your awareness again. William crosses the street, approaching you. But you at that moment can neither talk nor dialogue in peace; you cannot be wholly or positively attentive. Why? Because your consciousness has been stolen by the emotional upset of anger. It is as if your awareness were affected by the image and negative emotion recorded previously.

The other's purpose

When you adapt to the other's purpose and do not satisfy your own, you deny it. When the other feels whole and proud, they transmit their enthusiasm to you. It is an enthusiasm that soon dissolves, since it is not based on your path or your search for wholeness.

Often, as women traditionally 'have been' and 'have been represented' through men, they can continue with the tendency to abandon their aims, their personal characteristics, to join the male project. They leave their career, their women friends, their projects, to go off with him. For a man it is usually more difficult to take this step if it is the other way round, since for men, as we have seen, their self-esteem lies in their own professional projects.

'Selling oneself'

When the woman is submissive, needy and passive, she makes it easy for the man to take advantage of her. He satisfies his need to be the strong one and the protector. Then, on occasion, the woman reacts by getting angry. Alice submits to Peter's influence and desires. Then she realizes that he has taken advantage of her and she gets angry. A few days later they repeat the same pattern until in the end the relationship becomes parasitical.

It is necessary to rise up strongly from within and know how to say 'ENOUGH'.

If some clear limits are not set, women and men allow themselves to be manipulated, attracting relationships towards themselves that can end up becoming harmful.

In the relationship, one should decide if they want the other to possess them. In the development of the relationship, we begin by 'consuming' a pleasure. Then we move on from consuming to having, and we have a pleasure. From having we go to possessing: we possess the person that produces this pleasure in us. We use them. Finally we are what the other wants us to be so we can continue using them. That way we lose ourselves in the other's identity and disconnect from our essence.

For women, needs are more emotional than physical, but in order to 'snag' the man and 'not lose him' they will go to the physical, which means that they often lose their dignity. It is as if you were to sell your body and your soul to satisfy some deficiency through using the other. That way you destroy your self-respect. When dignity is lost, dissatisfaction appears.

Pleasure invades and traps the self in the senses and, for a time, the soul loses itself, absorbed in the pleasure, and appears to be satisfied. Then the existential void returns. It has been a passing pleasure. **The body cannot satisfy the deficiencies of the soul.**

Neither can the need to fill a lack be satisfied by 'giving yourself up' to someone whilst you are denying or hiding your own being. By repressing your personality in order to have someone, you cannot satisfy your true needs. If this happens, the emptiness and dissatisfaction increase.

It may be that the woman gives of herself honestly, but he often takes advantage of female neediness to satisfy his need for power, to be the strong one. She then feels guilty although she has not been able to control it, since her dependent need has allowed her to be carried away. There are fluctuations, rises and falls in the relationship. Our souls are burdened with senseless habits. We feed ourselves with the same 'waste' and do not break the loop.

Women usually adapt to and put up with things. They have more ability to stay and keep on going. But when the commitment is immature, more and more people stop tolerating it and separate; they want something new.

We live in a society that promotes novelty, even if it is super-fluous. It is a novelty of the season's fashions that have a sell-by date. Relationships have become liquid and also have a sell-by date. Although on the outside the person follows the fashion, on the inside their need and emptiness grow. It is like ingesting food that never nourishes you. You continue to be hungry.

The opportunity

In the face of a rupture, an abandonment, a separation, a disap-pointment or a crisis, you have the opportunity to go inside yourself, observe, revise and reinvent. To be honest with yourself and ask yourself: what are your needs, your aims, your desires, your feelings? Try not to project onto the other, don't stay stuck in the past experience, and think about yourself without blaming yourself. What can you do to become acceptably satisfied? Does your wholeness always depend on the other? No! It depends on you. You have to change something. You cannot go on waiting, thinking that he will change, that he (or she) is going through a process and when it is over, they will change. You should respect them and understand what you have to do. Begin by attending to your true needs.

I am told by James, a friend with two children aged five and seven, that his wife asked him for a separation and that he leave the home. In a few days he had lost what had taken him years to achieve: a flat in the city, a house in the mountains, a car, the furniture, etc. He was devastated by loneliness, disappointment, rejection and helplessness.

The moment at which a woman says 'that's enough', often the man loses his material possessions and, in a way, the possibility of a continued shared life with his children. He remains alone with himself. The tone of the relationship changes: you go from being partner and friend to being the enemy.

In most western countries women have achieved a greater legal protection than men when it comes to separation. Now in Australia the marriage laws are being changed to also support men.

In a few months, James entered into a spiritual awakening from which better things than those he had left have come to him. It was an opportunity to detach himself from the material and to grow spiritually. It did not happen overnight. First he had to find or remake his foundations. His commitment to his family was absolute, and, on finding himself 'in the street' he had to make new friendships, strengthen his social network and foster his work connections.

On many occasions, separation allows the man to get back his ability to be a father. Before, the woman invaded that space with such possessiveness that she did not allow the man, the father, in. I know many couples where this has occurred, given that after their separation the male has been more of a father than when they lived together as a couple. Sometimes it is because the father was absent. Other times because it was the mother who invaded those spaces of paternity.

After divorce, if one or both remain on their own, they can live this aloneness in many ways. Each one creates their reality. You can become aware of this and accept that this solitude is an opportunity to be with yourself. To reinvent yourself. It allows you to open up spaces of self-knowledge. You also open yourself up to other people from a more selfless place. It is a space of freedom in which you offer availability.

You are available to meet other people, to begin other friendships, to read and walk, to meditate and learn other arts. It is an availability that arises from a void, from a space that has been freed up. It depends on each person as to whether they fill this space with bad feelings or allow, and wait patiently for, healing, positive and transforming creativity to be born.

The empty creative space is that which you generate on letting go of dependences and cleaning out memories of the past. You cross a threshold and empty yourself of all that invades your inner space and makes you feel grief, fear and bitterness. You empty yourself of bad feelings to leave a clean space. On emptying yourself, you can feel that you are in the desert, unprotected from the elements, but on crossing it you empty yourself of the 'me' and of the possessive 'mine'. In this space, the presence of the purest and most subtle energy—intangible and invisible—can act, and thus there bursts forth in you an unlimited creativity. You are reborn.

Chapter 5

New Relationships

When we know who we are and what we want, relationships with others will become simpler and more natural for us.[1]
Wendy Bristow

The new way of love, which is true love (and is therefore not new but rather eternal), arises out of the meeting of two wholes and not out of the belief in or search for the union of two halves. Relationships are new when each member of the relationship connects to their essence, connects to their being, does their inner work, keeps up a rich personal dialogue and, in consequence, becomes a whole person who does not selfishly need the other in order to escape from themselves, but rather to complement them. Thus is created an option of peaceful and rich shared living in the present and for the future.

Approaching the encounter with the other from the wholeness of our eternal and spiritual being offers us a creative and complementary bond. As long as we go to the encounter of the other out of our dependent needs or our deficiencies, relationships will continue to be nests of conflicts and misunderstandings.

Understanding

Understanding is necessary in order to relate to the other without losing yourself in them. Understanding yourself, you know how to stay faithful to yourself and to your principles. That way, in the relationship with the other, you don't go against your principles. What does this faithfulness towards yourself mean? Faithful to what part of yourself? You can be faithful to what you would wish to be, or to your constant desire to be, faithful to what you have been, to a memory of yourself that you keep as a memory, like an image inside you. You can be faithful to an agreement or a way of acting. It is possible to be faithful to what you want to be and not to what you have been.

If you set out from an understanding of yourself you will be able to understand the other. Understanding helps you to maintain faithfulness and commitment to an agreement with yourself and with the other. When you understand your relationship with the other you will be able to understand your relationship to the whole, to society. The consequences of relating out of non-understanding are fighting, antagonism, confusion, infidelity, lack of union and duality.

Relating to the other out of personal understanding is the path to freedom, as Krishnamurti explains:[2]

When one understands oneself in their relationship to the other, the relationship does not become a process of isolation, but rather a movement that allows us to discover our own motives, our own thoughts, our own searches; and that discovery is the beginning of liberation and transformation. Only this immediate transformation can give rise to the fundamental, radical revolution which is so indispensable in the world. Revolution inside the walls of isolation is not revolution. The revolution comes only when the isolating walls are destroyed. This is only possible when one is no longer looking for power.

Valuing and loving oneself: reality or mirage?

New relationships should be based on a new form of valuing oneself: 'One can only love when one recognizes the singularity, the unique and unrepeatable quality of the other person. For this, one has to see them, value them, honor them as an individual and listen to them.'[3]

What is love in its moment of purity? Is it the moment when she feels raised to the category of Goddess? This happens when the woman feels that she has the man at her service, or, in other words, when the man is prepared to play her emotional game. In this game the most important moment is the one of emotional fusion. It is the most marvelous moment for the woman. Nevertheless, that is not love at its purest. It is an emotional passion in which, for some instants, separation disappears and there is a feeling of unity. That experience of union reminds us of the purity of the original union but it is a mirage because the point of departure is not pure love, but rather the dependent need of both.

Some women no longer expect this emotional fusion to last in a family, in children, but most of them would like it to be like that even if it can't be real. The desire for security and permanence is such that, when an emotional fusion occurs, the mind is triggered and projects the image of what it wants to see onto a fictitious reality.

There are more and more young men and women who do not see it like this and who accept the temporary nature of relationships. They experience a relationship as a chance for a fling, a liquid relationship. They find it hard to say no to a fling, not as a sexual contact, but rather as a romantic interlude of love.

To get beyond this illusion, this mirage, it is important to accept that the intensity of that passion is momentary. They are experiences which it perhaps does not make sense to want to always prolong nor to seek out continuously to renew. Learning not to get obsessed with this can open one to new horizons, new spaces, which have the potential to bring about conversations with other transformative contents. This way new possibilities are generated and other interests may be awakened.

There are many other interesting spheres to get passionate about. I get passionate about, amongst other things, art and creativity; service and dialogue; nature and beauty; music and dance. I get passionate about that which drives me to transcend.

So we have to reinvent love, building mature relationships. It is perhaps the first time that we are in a position to be able to ask ourselves about these ideas, seriously and democratically, not only as the experience of an elite. In the following chapters, I will continue to look in depth at the energy of love, at pure love, *agape*.

Love relationships need to reconstruct the masculine gender and the feminine. This present-day adventure, of 'disposable' relationships, is heartbreaking and exhausting, given that many of them end up being destructive.

Relationships are lasting and enriching when each one has personal security independently of whether the other meets their needs or not. Rather than expectations, there is acceptance.

A lot of inner security is required in order to give oneself up to the love of another person. The security of the man that comes from a foundation of a nourished, renewed and spiritual masculinity is still an attribute that has to be developed in our cultural model.

In the encounter between a man and a woman, there is the amalgam of the authentic and deep masculine and the essential and deep feminine. If it is not like that, what occurs is loneliness. They are relationships of mutual empowerment. It is not the case that one takes energy and the other discharges themselves and weakens. A pure energy is incorporated into the situation that alters the established model, in such a way that it allows light to be spread in new ways, ways that are still to be discovered.

Two meet and there is unity in the relationship. They seem to be one. Not a diminished and enclosed one but a one that is open to the world. The self that loves gives itself to the loved 'you', in such a way that it no longer wants to be self, but that 'you'.

However, the reality is that nobody will ever completely fulfill us. That person, like us, is also deprived and lacking in something. These deficiencies are precisely what revitalize the desire and search for more transcendental forms of union until we reach total union. For a relationship to be constructive, each one should keep on working on him or herself and looking into the inner mirror of their heart.

Partners, companions on the path, team, friendship

In the new relationships, we are partners on the path. Each walks the route of the path using their own feet, that is, they walk it alone. But they are together with a companion who they lean on, with whom they share, hold dialogue, reflect and, thus, the experience of the journey is enriched. In this way we grow together.

We can join forces and make a team, supporting each other and playing together at the game of life. Each has their role and function in the team, but we share the same hope. We have a vision that unites us.

The value of friendship enriches the meaning of your life. Devote time to cultivating friendship. The relationships with your friends accompany you in your good and bad times. A friend can be a beacon in the darkness that points you at that moment to where you are and where you are going or want to go to.

The new relationships are those in which we add up, and together, we are better. We stop comparing, competing, criticizing and feeling jealous. We co-operate, unite, value and support. We are partners in order to create a better reality for everyone.

One of the aspects that prevents us from creating and living this mutual supportiveness is the fundamental instinct to protect our individual self and be ourselves. That is why we try not to feel invaded, attacked, bothered or dominated by others. This leads us to want to defend ourselves and to move within a defined individual space. That is why we sometimes reject others and, with our attitudes, send messages like: 'Don't come close, don't bother me'. This in the end has the effect of our finding ourselves alone and isolated.

On living together with others, we have not learned that the important space that we should know, connect to and define is the inner space. When the inner space of being is cultivated, we are aware that nobody can take away from us what we are or our inner qualities: then we can feel comfortable amongst the multitude and we do not feel that we have to defend our space.

The ego tries to defend its spaces; that is why some people prefer to work alone and feel that teamwork is uncomfortable. When you take away the ego's armor, you don't need to defend anything. What you are, you are. Nobody can take it away from you or destroy it. In this way, you meet one of the most basic needs of every human being: that of belonging. We can belong to a group, a family, a team or a community. Some feel comfortable being a team player; others prefer to sit on the sideline and watch the players.

On belonging to a team, you are present; you participate and collaborate with others. This participation is able to inspire and motivate in a way that is unthinkable for a person on their own. It is those who live and work with others who have the inner power, not those who distance themselves from others. For others we do things that we would not do for ourselves.

If you decide to overcome your self-limitations you will be able to participate better in the game. To do so, put yourself in a place where you feel uncomfortable, and, on going through this discomfort, you will undergo an extraordinary process of learning about yourself. Widen your limits, open yourself to new horizons and you will become aware of your possibilities.

In the end, you will be able to be a team player, on your own, or an observer, depending on the need and the moment.

Each time that someone bothers you, or you feel invaded or upset by their presence, you can go within and change your attitude. Watch: what is happening when you are intolerant? Whenever you feel an emotional disturbance it means that you have separated from the center of your being, which is stable, strong and calm. In that moment, try to see that it is offering you an opportunity instead of feeling that someone is a problem.

In shared living, you develop and practice your qualities: tolerance, capacity of adaptation, of listening, understanding, forgiving, communicating, flowing, discerning, not being influenced and not depending. That way you learn to be yourself when amongst others. Do not be you when you are alone and 'another' when you are with others. In this authenticity lies your integrity, tranquillity and self-esteem.

As Branden[4] explains:

True self-esteem is how we feel about ourselves when things do not go well. This means when we are challenged by the unexpected, when others do not agree with us, when we find ourselves without resources, when the shelter of the group cannot protect us any longer from the tasks and risks of life, when we have to think, choose, decide and act and nobody guides us or applauds us. At these moments our deepest premises are revealed. One of the biggest lies that we have ever been told is that it is 'easy' to be selfish and that sacrifice implies spiritual strength. When in fact people sacrifice themselves thousands of times a day, even against their own conscience. This is their tragedy. Respecting oneself — respecting one's own mind, criteria, values and convictions — is the ultimate act of bravery. We see how rare it is. But it is what self-esteem demands of us.

Agreements

Some agreements will help us to maintain mutual support, trust and fluid dialogue. Don Miguel Ruiz[5] suggests these four agreements based on the ancient Toltec wisdom:

1. Be impeccable with your words. Speak with integrity. Say only what you mean. Use the power of your word with

authenticity and love.

2. Do not take anything personally, this is also a key from the Tao. What others do is not because of you nor against you. What others say and do is a projection of their own reality, their dreams and mirages. If you become immune to other's opinions, you will not fall victim to useless suffering in relationships.

3. Do not make suppositions nor draw conclusions about everything too quickly. On doing so, you believe that what you suppose is true and you create a reality about it. It is not always positive or guided by love. Have the courage to ask, clarify and express what you want. Communicate with others as clearly as you can in order to avoid misunderstandings, sadness and other dramas. With only this agreement you can transform your life completely.

4. Always try to do the most and the best you can. And what is best is going to change from moment to moment. It will be different, for example, depending on whether you are ill or well. Under any circumstance, do it as best as you can and that way you will avoid blaming yourself, judging yourself and pitying yourself.

Listening

You need courage to get up and speak. You need courage to sit down and listen.
Winston Churchill

On many occasions women ask to be listened to but not given advice or judged by their companions. Listened to from spaces of intimacy, tenderness and love. Women are grateful if they can share with a man who can listen to them without interrupting them, and who does not feel obliged to give them answers and solutions.

When you listen and advise out of the need to rescue, you prevent something wiser and cleaner from arising in the other person and in you. When you want to 'save' another and help them, sometimes you fall into that rescue state and empty yourself of energy. That way you help neither the other nor yourself.

Women also ask to be able to hear what they want or need to listen to, not what men need to say or express. When men begin to open themselves to their emotional world, as they can or know how to, in order to discover something that they themselves do not know, they need our understanding and support. On listening to them out of neediness, we do not make the change easy for them.

The patriarchal paradigm has poisoned all of us and we should detoxify ourselves together. Sometimes, in the expression there is a healthy emotional opening, but on other occasions what is expressed is an outburst of suffocated and repressed energies. We show our inability to transform ourselves by putting outside what we should resolve within.

This leads us to consider the importance of listening to yourself first. You do not need to 'share out' your emotional waste. Meditate, work on yourself within and transform. That way what you express will come out of your light, and if it does come out of your shadow, it won't do so as a great outburst but out of the responsibility of someone who takes on board what they feel.

The listening should be initiated in the inner dialogue about your true emotional needs, your feelings, in order to reach an understanding as to what your essential desire and your most intimate longing is. What really moves, motivates and inspires you.

Chapter 6

Partners in Complementarity

For there to be complementarity in relationships it is important to move away from the competitive paradigm that fosters violence, duality and separation. The masculinity that is governed by power, victory, triumph and aggressiveness can only ever be dualistic, since it recognizes some attributes and excludes its opposites. It demands courage *without* fear, strength *without* vulnerability, victory *without* concessions.[1]

The complementarity between masculine and feminine is natural, and, when it takes place, there is order. Neediness disappears. For it to take place with the other, first it should happen in oneself. This is the *yin* and *yang* in the Chinese tradition. The *Anima* and the *Animus* of Carl Jung. Or Shiva and Shakti in the Hindu tradition, where we also find Vishnu, with the four arms that symbolize the integration of the masculine and the feminine in oneself.

First you have to find this wholeness in yourself. Experience the original femininity, the *yin*, and the original masculinity, the *yang*, in yourself. That way you will be able to enter into a relationship with the other in which there will not be co-dependence, but rather complementarity.

When the man–woman relationship is founded only on the instinct, it has a bodily relationship, not mental, emotional or spiritual. The instincts dominate and the person does not think clearly. The intuition is blocked. There is not complementarity, but rather dualism. Ways of union are sought through sex, attachment, submission and force. As a result, there is disunity, pain, fear and sadness.

When two people join together as complete beings or as people who are working on themselves in order to reach that state, the relationship is more than the sum of both parts. There is parity and respect. In any relationship, the basis of harmony is respect. If you respect yourself you will be able to respect even the one who does not respect you. You will not need to defend yourself, justify yourself or attack.

If, on the contrary, both of them are needy and dependent, and one tries to meet their need through the other, and vice versa, in the end this does not work. The taking from the other does not really meet the inner need, and the dissatisfaction continues to be there. Ties are created instead of relationships.

Building a relationship requires effort on both sides. We have been made to think that it is possible to be happy without the effort of overcoming, without the tension of commitment, without the mastery of the self, without the greatness of rectification.

Being honest and sincere is also one of the bases of complementarity. Avoid false diplomacy. Put your deficiencies on the table and let the other receive them with understanding and acceptance. In complementarity, you accept the other as they are and you encourage them to be as they could come to be. You receive their defects and inspire them so that they might transform them along the way as you also are working on your shadows. We don't have to be in agreement to love one another. You express and share. Dialogue flows.

Let us learn the art of loving, of being free and allowing the other to be. Pure love is an unconditional love that flows freely, is healing and never wounds. You give yourself to the other. It is a giving of oneself in which there is a giving up of the self. You transcend your 'ego-self' without however losing yourself or getting stuck onto the other. To reach that state in a relationship it is necessary to have a certain maturity and to have evolved on a personal level. Most people love one another and tie one another down. When freedom is lost, happiness goes, and the well-being gives way to unhappiness.

Knowledge of oneself facilitates the process of going from fear to a form of loving that is richer, more tolerant and relaxed. Emotional love can turn into true love as the initial fire of the emotions cools and is substituted by a wiser and more mature perception. True love needs a fresh and renewing atmosphere, without fears.

To free ourselves of the tendency towards dependence, we should have a strong heart, capable of renouncing its selfishness; a heart that has nothing to hide and that, therefore, leaves the mind free and without any fear; a heart that is always ready to accept new information and change its mind, that does not cling on to closed beliefs or obsolete data.

With a worried mind and closed heart we cannot see and receive new ideas, opportunities or people in our life. Let's learn to let go of the past, to forgive and forget, to live in this moment the wholeness of our heart of light, a heart that cultivates good feelings, without bitterness. Cultivating the true values—peace, serenity, love, freedom and solidarity—we will overcome our deficiencies, we will feel stronger. A heart like that ends up transforming into a lamp that dispels the darkness.

A heart like that lives in the now. The return to the 'now' means to embrace what you are and welcome in the present moment. Usually you shape your expectations according to situations and people. However, you can shape your life, be open to receive it. When you receive, you give, you give 'yourself' and in the giving of your self you receive again. In this reciprocity a dance of joy is created.

Let us dance in the complicity of creating relationships that strengthen us and connect us to our true identity, relationships that flow in the dance of joy and are not a battle involving great suffering. From our being we will be able to embrace each other in the creation of a world where love and peace reign. But from what being? What is our identity?

Identity

'Know yourself' is a phrase sculpted over the entrance to Apollo's temple in Delphos, Greece. Knowing yourself has nothing to do with the beliefs or ideas that float around in your mind. It is to be rooted in your being without feeling lost in the mind or the body, in roles or labels. It implies a process of un-identification with all of this in order to re-find your essence.

The problem of identifying ourselves with our gender is that, as women, we are at the same time moulded and led (consciously or unconsciously) by what for millennia it has meant to be a 'woman' in its positive, impressive, sense and in its limiting and destructive sense. As men, we are 'intoxicated' by what it has meant to be a man for millennia.

If we want to know how to change our thinking and transform our acts; if we want to feel strong in order to live the life we want to live for ourselves and for our world, it is essential to connect to our identity free of limiting conditioning and open to our true being.

The original identity of the being, of consciousness, is free of gender conditioning. It is an identity without a gender. However, when we 'inhabit' the body, we receive the projections and education connected to gender and what it means to be a woman and a man. We will look at the subject of identity as it is connected to gender.

Female identities

Your sense of being

When we put our sense of being in what we do or what we have, we become dependent and vulnerable. The problem does not lie in having money, possessions, jobs, people, or properties, but rather in our identification with them. Strangely, women have tried to 'be someone' by following in male footsteps: having a career, professional achievements, a good salary, a flat or a house, etc. All this offers us the autonomy and the freedom that we were deprived of for so long. The problem comes when we identify with it and our being is lost in the doing and the having.

Then, on restricting yourself to a limited identity, you narrow your viewpoint, you diminish and imprison yourself. In so doing, you give up your power and freedom to the object of your identification (be it a person, the body, a role, a position or a place). When those objects change, your self-esteem, confidence and self-respect collapse.

When your happiness starts depending on what the other does, your emotional state goes up and down like a yoyo. When the meaning of who you are is defined by your image, your husband, your wife, your friendships, your house, your money, your reputation, your work, in the end you lose the meaning of who you are. All of this can disappear tomorrow. Then, where are you? Who are you?

Woman's role in the new family units

It seems that society in general has not taken much interest in the role that women are playing in the new family units. As a single mother, the woman multiplies her activity without stopping work. As the wife of a man who has children that are not hers, it is up to her to play mother when they are ill, to be the stepmother in order to exercise authority, housemaid when she enters the kitchen, friend when an accomplice is required, wife to balance the home. That is, that woman is everything, even if she continues to be nothing.

Caroline Ward, in her book *The Four Faces of Woman*, develops the faces, traditional, modern, eternal and the face of woman's power (the Shakti, the Goddess). I use these denominations here, since they seem appropriate to the subject we are dealing with.

Traditional identity

The traditional woman renounces her right to decide for herself in exchange for security. She assures herself of being welcomed, accepted and therefore safe. She tries to please and look good. She does not put the norms of the clan into question. She accepts the rules and the cultural conditioning that defines them. She feels secure under rules and insecure without them. She lives in a closed system of 'secure' beliefs. Security is what drives her. She needs to belong to a strong man who offers her security. If she does not find that man, she becomes part of a group and makes an effort to be accepted, loved, approved of and supported by the members of the group or by the hierarchy of the same. She limits herself out of fear of leaving her children in an unprotected situation, and above all, out of the fear of loneliness. The risk of freedom is precisely that: loneliness.

To feel secure, it is difficult, at times almost impossible, for her to think outside of the limits that have been defined for her over time. She does not pay attention to her inner voice, her conscience, and, in consequence, she damages her ability to discern and make decisions.

She clings. It is devastating for her to lose what was and what has always been. And, as loss is inevitable, as nothing is permanent, the result is sadness. She is often sad. She lives with the fear of loss and is sad when she loses.

Modern identity

The modern face of woman questions narrow-minded mentality, confronts hierarchy and begins revolutions.

Valeriane Bernard tells us that, when a woman realizes that she has lost herself in the tradition of others; when she feels that who she intrinsically is has been erased; when she no longer knows what she feels or believes; when she perceives that she has neither the power nor the freedom to be who she is; when she awakens to the fact that she has simply adopted the thoughts and opinions of her parents, her partner, or the given stereotypes, to a greater or lesser degree, her anger will emerge, ranging from being upset to getting absolutely furious.[2]

Woman, in her modern identity, is radicalized. She imposes feminism onto the patriarchy. She seeks to regain the lost power. She challenges the rules of the clan. She rejects them. This brings about an opposite reaction in men. These latter reaffirm themselves in their sexist ways. The feminists and the sexist men attack each other and continue in this battle, not moving away from the toxicity that invades them. They perpetuate duality.

Leadership in this modern face seeks power 'up there'. When people arrive there, if they do, they realize that the power capable of transforming isn't to be found up there. It is a key. The power is divine and it is inside you. It is Shakti.

In her modern identity, woman becomes a transgressor and does not accept the male law. From the transgression, she ends up on her own in an absence of love. She has used the same weapons of the game as in the male toxicity that invades the system. Finally, the fighting woman, when she realizes that in reality she hasn't transformed anything, may feel despondent, hopeless, and exhausted.

She is very focused on the future. She devotes a disproportionate amount of mental energy digressing into thoughts about the how, the what, the why and the when. She finds it difficult to relax, enjoy the present day. She forgets the art of living.

If, as women, we continue to react against the system, we have not yet found the road back to ourselves. Let us change the system and the control mechanisms, but out of our inner power and our essence, not out of rejection and repulsion. Let's offer alternatives.

The modern face can misunderstand authenticity and independence by living out of an arrogant autonomy that even rejects God. In religious contexts, on the other hand, there can be an influence so that the person believes that it is the will of God for one to become the instrument that radiates divine light onto the new contemporary path.

Eternal identity

This identity is the beginning and the end of our path. It is the sacred condition of our being. The essential being, without defenses, without masks, without cracks. It is the state of 'I am', without doubts, confusion or duality. Being out of respect for oneself. Being with sureness and humility. Being without the need to prove anything to anybody. Pure energy, without mixtures, shadows or uncertainties. Complete clarity and balance. It is the creative being that experiences the original art of living.

The eternal identity shows an innocent face, with openness and natural curiosity. It has its presence in the now. As Plato said: 'The one who is able to find the path on the cutting edge of the moment, will catch a glimpse of eternity.'

The eternal identity connects us to the Goddess. I will expand on this theme in the section 'The Goddesses' in chapter 8.

Neediness begins when we stop believing in the marvelous nature of this sacred being and start to believe in alien formulas.

Male identities

Traditionally, man is resistant, assertive, enterprising, aggressive and impulsive. He is strong, decisive and has courage. He takes risks and wins. His ambition is unlimited. He is a provider, protector, producer, savior; he is powerful. He flaunts the power of controlling. In essence, he is king.

Independence and autonomy are characteristics of a male identity. What happens is that, often, these turn into an isolation, above all emotional, in which the communication is of external, not internal, facts and matters. The inner world is kept hidden. There is a dissociation with the emotional. Perhaps he will manage to speak about some feelings, but he will express them with difficulty. That is, the most he will do is limit himself to talking about them, not expressing them.

Given that this is a socially imposed cultural model, we do

find discrepancies. There are, luckily, men who do not adhere to what is prescribed and who fight to be who they are, free of the restrictions imposed on them by the system.

Man can and should re-find himself with his healthy masculine part in order to personify the new man. He has the key to going forwards. He can contribute much more than simply going from being a sexist model to being a politically correct man who cleans at home, looks after the child, is praised by his partner and backed up by society. The change that is necessary is deeper, more at the root. It means a change in values, attitudes and behavior. A fundamental change in beliefs about what it is to be a man.

As Marina Subirats says, the question for men is: 'What to do with all the baggage of value and bravery that they had to accumulate in order to reach the level of their true role?'[3]

Eternal masculinity

In the eternal masculinity, man gets back his inner power. To be a man he does not need to prove himself, overcome nor triumph. He expresses a mature masculinity, with its own emotional and spiritual roots. In this state, it is possible to establish a relationship of complementarity with a woman. It will be more feasible if she is also deeply rooted in her inner power and her eternal feminine (which I looked at in the previous section).

For men, this task is urgent: to accept their world of feelings and not feel themselves to be less of a man for it. Robert Moore, doctor in psychology and theologian, and Douglas Gillette, founder of the Institute for World Spirituality in Chicago, say that we have come to 'think that feelings and, in particular, "our" feelings, are bothersome and inappropriate obstacles when it comes to being men'.[4]

When a man learns to see himself in the wholeness of his being, he is loving and knows how to love. Out of that awareness, he finds a meeting point with a woman by setting out from a different place: it does not arise out of the conquering 'macho' who fears giving of himself and emotional intimacy, but out of the open and understanding being that knows how to commit itself with sincerity. He takes on board that in commitment there is complementarity and enrichment. He knows how to have a woman at his side as a person with all the same rights, obligations and needs as him, without feeling jealous of her professional achievements, her intelligence or her brilliance.

He knows that being male is not synonymous with being the most intelligent, the strongest or the most powerful. He is aware that **power is not lost when it is shared**; that decisions taken together are easier to make; that sharing the care of his children is fundamental in his role as a father; that being cold does not make him more virile; that men express themselves and cry… and that's fine. It is a manhood that is spiritually fertile and emotionally developed. It is a masculinity sustained by the strength of love, the courage of the spirit and commitment and the bravery of compassion.[5]

Chapter 7

Partners to Live in Wholeness

Rooted in your identity, the steps towards shared living in wholeness are those explained below.

Change your perception

It is possible to experience situations without becoming emotionally spent. This does not mean that you have to become cold or insensitive towards what is happening around you. It is a question of living through situations without burying oneself in them. If you drown in them you will not be able to help anybody, not even yourself. You will be lost like a shipwreck at the mercy of the waves. You will have lost control over the helm of your boat, your life.

The question lies in knowing what the strategy is in order to learn to live through situations without them determining your emotional and mental state. It is about living without allowing circumstances to create that unhappiness, stress, suffering, sadness, frustration and anger in your life.

To achieve this, first you should change your interpretation. Instead of seeing the fact as an obstruction, interference or barrier on your path, interpret it as an opportunity to grow. You might find it easier if you ask yourself, for example: what has this situation taught me? What signals is it giving me? Watch and listen before immediately reacting. Out of observation and listening you can have a more objective and wider perception.

Reality in itself does not cause stress, pain or unhappiness. Our perception and interpretation of reality causes these reactions. Therefore, we have to revise how we perceive situations and with what beliefs we interpret and judge them.

Reinterpreting the situation, the specific reality, means

allowing the old perception to die to make room for a new vision. If the old does not die, the new cannot be correctly built.

Instead of seeing people or situations as obstacles on the path, you can see them as opportunities. They offer you the possibility of stopping and observing yourself; of practicing patience and tolerance; of improving your listening; of being grateful and loving. They give you the opportunity to detach yourself and stand at a healthy distance in order to see objectively. They help you to reconsider your objectives. They allow you to extend your ability to co-operate and expand your heart so that you are more generous.

To have a wider perception and not drown in the situation, you can position yourself in a better way. If you stabilize yourself in self-respect, in maintaining your self-esteem and a healthy distance (not necessarily physical, more to do with not letting the situation absorb you), you will be able to have an eagle's view. From above, everything looks smaller. It is much easy to get over something small. You can.

Whatever happens, it is important to always be aware that you create your thoughts and you allow the images of the situations you experience to have a greater or lesser impact within you, depending on how you internalize it. Learn to create thoughts full of love, courage, trust and determination. Those thoughts charged with positive energy will help you to allow each situation to happen, to really overcome it and leave it behind, for it not to stay alive in your thoughts or your memory.

With the power of a mind that creates thoughts full of good and concentrated energy, wherever you go, you will create a pleasant atmosphere. Your vibrations will emanate and create spaces and situations full of beauty, trust and tranquillity, spaces where all those entering into them will let down their defenses and connect again with the authenticity of their being.

Meet needs or transcend them?

Dissatisfaction prevents you from savoring wholeness. Dissatisfaction arises from—and at the same time produces—dependence, frustration, even anger and violence. The question lies in whether you have to find out how to meet your needs or whether you need to transcend those that are, or you consider to be, unnecessary. Transcend the desires that distract you from the essential search. Set aside what causes you unnecessary anxiety because you are trying to satisfy what at bottom will continue to leave you dissatisfied. In order to set it aside, you should be careful that it doesn't attract you. That which attracts you ends up trapping you and absorbing you, in such a way that, although you want to set it aside, you won't be able to. In silence, with the practice of meditation, you are attracted to the essential. That way you manage to set aside the unnecessary. You leave it behind and you go forward.

From separation to union

A reality exists that we as human beings should face: separation. The fundamental separation was when we separated from our 'home', from our incorporeal state, in the *brahm* element, the element of light, the space of nirvana, beyond sound, beyond movement. It is a space of eternity in which we are beyond action and reaction. The soul inhabits it, without body, in peace, next to God.

The following separation is that of the maternal body where we gestated and from which we had to disconnect. And finally, the division of genders. The soul is neither masculine nor feminine; when it takes on a body the separation of gender takes place, with all the cultural, educational, religious and social weight that this implies.

After these separations, the human being never gives up trying to unite, to leave behind duality and to return to the union, the One. Love is the energy and the power that, like a magnet, pushes us towards this union. It joins us between genders, it joins us to humanity and the universe, and it joins us to our original state of light, to our divine essence. 'We are made of incompleteness,' says Javier Melloni, 'in order to find wholeness beyond ourselves.'[1] 'We have to transcend our self-ego in order to re-find the lost union. Through relationship and joy, we can connect to it. We don't always get it back. In the silence of contemplation, *agape* emerges, the unconditional love that joins us to the whole beyond ourselves.'

In the steps towards the satisfaction of desire we can take two roads: one that takes us to the outside, to the search for connection with the other, with otherness. Another one takes us within, to discover that what we look for outside is to be found in oneself: in the essential being, in the soul.

Meditation and contemplation make up part of this second option: going within. Meditation calms you and opens up the path to re-finding yourself in your essence. In the experience of inner silence you realize that many apparent needs are not really so. They are *maya*, false mirages, impulses based on a selfish starting point, limited and small. In the silence of being, you connect to what you really want, you look for and give meaning to your path through life.

Accept

Accepting yourself is the key to beginning and carrying out any positive change. It means approving of yourself and giving yourself the seal of approval. While you are rejecting a part of yourself, you cannot fully know enjoyment. A duality exists within you. However many other areas of confidence you enjoy, on rejecting yourself you wound your self-esteem. This weakens you.

When you reject the pain that you feel, thinking that something in you is failing, you expand the problem. The knowledge of what is happening to you has to be followed by acceptance. Tolle states:

> To accept means that you allow yourself to feel what you are
> feeling at that moment. It forms part of the essence of now.
> You cannot argue against what is. If you do, you suffer. On
> accepting it, you become what you are: vast, spacious. You
> become complete. You are no longer a fragment, which is how
> the ego perceives itself. Your true nature emerges, which is at
> one with the nature of God.[2]

To accept yourself is to feel that you are in the right place, at the right time, doing what is right. Out of acceptance, you have changed certain beliefs. Before, you believed that you had to act as if you were strong in order to go out into the world; now you are in the world and you show yourself as you are, not needing to prove anything. Before, you had a feeling of little self-value; now you know where it comes from, you know there is no reason to have it and you no longer feel inferior. You feel better.

You accept yourself and you express yourself by generating a space of acceptance for others who, in your presence, feel accepted, embraced and comfortable.

Out of the space of acceptance a different action is created. An action that respects, joins together, opens, calms and embraces.

To accept the other is to allow them to be without armor and express themselves without fears. It is easier to say this than to practice it. Specifically, when you have expectations placed in your friend or companion, and they disappoint you, it is difficult for you to accept.

After a separation, acceptance facilitates you with the path to free yourself of disappointment and suffering. The other was not as you would have liked. The relationship has unleashed a series of unpleasant reactions and situations. You feel them to be 'unacceptable'.

It is necessary to accept the feelings that you cannot deal with:

rejection, insecurity, envy, rage, fear, disapproval. Imagine how you would feel if you did not resist this feeling but rather accepted it fully. Try it now. The situation that caused the feeling has perhaps already passed, but you cling on to it and on top of that, you reject it, you hide it or run from it, which means that you keep it, and it grows inside you until you burst or get ill.

What was, was, and has passed. It no longer is. It is no longer there. Everything is in continuous change. Permanence is illusory. Clinging out of fear of change is harmful. The temporary nature of comings and goings, in relationships, in support and props, makes up part of the law of life. Nothing is permanent. The supports are temporary. If you accept this, you free yourself.

Forgive

If you don't forgive the other, your energy is dispersed. You think a lot and you cannot control your feelings; you feel rage, anger and frustration. Your mind and heart are contaminated by the inner noise, and suffering invades you. Often you keep bitterness in your heart because you have not forgiven. Sometimes, when it is a matter of a broken heart, it is not only a question of forgiving the other, but also of forgiving yourself for having allowed yourself to enter into that experience. At the end of the day, you took the step that allowed you to go into that relationship in the way that you did. If you hadn't taken that step, you wouldn't have had that experience. You accepted that challenge, that relationship, and what might happen in it. Therefore, you don't only have to learn to forgive the other, but also to forgive yourself.

On one occasion a man took advantage of me; he deceived me and swindled me. When I realized, I couldn't believe how naive I had been. How did I allow that man to lie to me like that? How did I believe and trust in him? Am I so stupid? These thoughts tortured me. Until I realized that I had to forgive myself. To learn the lesson, but not to continue tormenting myself for the experience I had had. The fact of forgiving myself freed me.

When I met him by accident after some time, I was able to look him in the eyes.

Guilt is a burden that prevents you from forgiving yourself. It is much easier to forgive the other than to forgive yourself.

Agape is divine love; it is a selfless love that does not seek return and that is related to the capacity to forgive. When you forgive, you love.

Reconcile

In the face of differences and conflict, we tend to have defensive attitudes of confrontation. We argue; we do not dialogue. We blame and attack, we do not take responsibility. We align ourselves with those that defend our positions of confrontation. This separates and distances us. The conflict gets worse. Society is more and more polarized. We live in duality.

To get beyond these confrontations we would have to change method and seek reconciliation. To reconcile with the other is to reconcile with yourself. That way you get closer to peace and you make dialogue possible.

It is also necessary to reconcile yourself with your purpose. Not to run from your destiny. Listening, observing and reconciling yourself with who you are is to accept yourself, open yourself and to shine. To reconcile yourself with your goal and your purpose is to put them into practice, taking the necessary steps for them to be fulfilled. Without running, without denying, without complaining, and, with perseverance, advancing.

To meet our needs, as both women and men we have to reconcile ourselves with the eternal feminine and with the eternal masculine, that is, with the essential being deeply rooted in our inner power (as we have seen in the sections 'Eternal identity' and 'Eternal masculinity'). That which is in you, in me, and in each one of us. We should open up to it without fear so that it can come to the surface with all its truth, goodness and beauty.

Embrace uncertainty

When you question yourself as to how you have been living to date and your beliefs start to seem a bit limited to you, it is a sign that you are changing. Something is breaking inside you. You feel uncertainty and perhaps feel like crying: what you used to lean on no longer gives you support and you find yourself faced with emptiness and loneliness. You know that you have to let go, but you can't find anywhere to hold on to.

In the first place, you shouldn't be alarmed; it is a good sign when this rupture happens inside you! Don't be afraid! Remember that life is energy in constant change, and nothing stays fixed: we live through birth and death several times within. You have to be prepared to be reborn and allow all that is no longer of any use to you to die.

Value what has been of use to you until now, and when you no longer need it, have the ability to let go, let it go, thus creating space to embrace the new. You feel that it is a challenge because you have to take a leap into the void, as you don't know what really awaits you. You find yourself without support. Your beliefs and habits seem limited. You need to breathe new air to help you in this new phase you are beginning.

It is the opportunity to revise your dreams: what is it that your soul really longs to reach? Remember that your creative capacity is extraordinary; trust yourself and cultivate your inner resources in order to get closer to your aims. Creativity, flexibility and trust are the key to living through this rupture with the old, the past, and accepting the new, the unknown, the uncertain. Look for a creativity that allows you to visualize and realize your purpose, approaching your ideal in a novel way.

Find the flexibility necessary to adapt to changes. Trust that everything will go well. That way you will get to know other facets of yourself and you will become aware of the great potential that you still have to awaken within you. You will find new support and new friendships. Other opportunities will appear and you will glimpse new horizons that will set off your enthusiasm and motivation.

Detach yourself and let go

The man that lets go of the pride of possession, free of the feeling of the 'I' and of what is 'mine', reaches supreme peace.
Bhagavad Gita 2, 71

To detach oneself is to go back, to take a step backwards in order to expand your vision. To look at a painting, you cannot stick your nose in it; you go backwards and, from a distance, you see it better and you enjoy it more. Anthony Strano, in his book *Los cuatro movimientos naturales*, defines it thus: 'When there is confusion, pain or a lack of clarity it begins to be useful to take a step back. Often we cannot see the habitual behavior that affects and harms us. Stepping back provides us with a neutral space so as to discern how and where to navigate our boat.'

We need to be brave in order to let go of our attachments on a mental and emotional level. It is a question of strengthening the courage to maintain our detachment, especially when outside pressures (generally other people) and inner forces (our personal habits) incite us to cling on, to depend and to attach ourselves again. Freeing oneself from suffering is not achieved with the desire to be free, which is a way of clinging on to a concept of freedom. Freedom comes when you put an end to the clinging. It means to cut oneself off from or stop identifying with the image of the object one is clinging to. By object I am referring to something external, be it things, people, places, or rather something internal, such as ideas, beliefs or memories.

When you learn to let go, you realize that you are on the road to true freedom. You recognize to what extent you had become attached. You stop depending and attaching yourself, not clinging on to anything, not even ideas, stories, situations, possessions, habits, or personality traits. You find yourself in an open space, an inner space without borders, without limits, without objects. There is peace in that space. You are aware of the connection between all things. In that space lives love, and from it love springs up and expresses itself.

To detach oneself also means knowing how to detach yourself from doing. If you are tangled up in doing, in a variety of actions and in being constantly on the go, at some moment something will go wrong in your life. Learn to regain energy and not only to spend it and wear yourself out. Brake in order not to crash. If you don't brake, life puts the brake on for you with an accident, a death, an illness or a twisted ankle.

Even if you are satisfied with the achievements and the successes of what you do, a moment will come when you feel a void or an inner deficiency. Doing is not the complete way of fulfilling yourself. Wholeness is an energetic state, plethoric, but peaceful and calmed. However many successes one has, these achievements do not fully fill the being. External success will never create complete inner satisfaction.

For example, actors, singers and concert players, after much applause for their performance, return home or to their hotel and can be invaded by a bitter loneliness and a sensation of emptiness. Receiving applause for a good performance can never substitute the satisfaction afforded by a good friendship or a meditation centered on your essential being, stripped of the 'character'. On detaching yourself, you can observe your dependences. You can see that you need approval in order to go forward. Allow yourself the freedom to think and act as you would like without needing the other to approve of you. Approve of yourself. You can.

Detachment is to give out of inner abundance. Cultivating and nourishing the self, you can offer yourself without fears. You offer yourself out of abundance, not out of your deficiencies and fear.

Observe and revise

Become an observer for a few minutes. Watch your mind: observe the thoughts, control their speed, their criticisms, their anger, their stress. Slow them down. As you retreat from your mind and your situation, things take on another perspective and you begin to feel peace.
Anthony Strano

Observe the patterns that are repeated in your day to day and in your life. Find out what you keep them going for and perhaps they will give you the key as to why you continue in neediness.

Seeing yourself within requires an effort of introspection. Communicating with oneself is the first step towards bringing harmony to any discomfort. When communication with others is not fluid, and emotions of anger, bitterness, rage and fear erupt, the inner dialogue brings harmony and heals. When moodiness and unease take over you, the first step is to observe yourself: what is the matter with you, how do you feel, who is ruling your mind? Look at yourself without blaming others and without thinking about them. Observe this present moment and describe what you feel. You can write it down.

Observe; you shouldn't blame anybody, because the difficulty begins and ends in you. As Strano confirms:

Others simply reflect what you refuse to acknowledge in yourself. You cannot evade yourself eternally. The mirror of time reflects reality, which demands its presence. You stop blaming and accusing, you avoid the temptation of falling into despair, of isolating yourself and justifying your 'reasons'. You no longer seek the support of those who bless your indignation. You are prepared, with all the courage and humility you are capable of, to accept that it is now time that 'I change'.[3]

On observing and accepting, you feel the presence of the observer. The inner being, the one that observes, has enough resources to redirect thoughts, use their strong points and change the direction of negative and weak thoughts, transcending sadness, anger and fear.

When you connect to the authenticity of what you really are, you re-find your serenity: you stop the repetitive thoughts that make you unhappy. You realize that, when you project yourself onto others and you blame them for your anger, believing they have wounded you, you allow yourself to be enslaved and to be their victim. Watching and realizing is the first step in redirecting the course of your attitudes and your reactions.

Watch and ask yourself: what has happened to you? Where have you gone wrong? Revise in order to find the keys to the change that you need; don't revise in order to blame others or yourself. Don't do it in order to find out where or how the other made an error. Don't judge them, given that you don't know all their history. Don't run from the mirror of your heart and contemplate yourself in it. Don't run from your inner noises. Listen to the tide. Listen to yourself.

Renounce. Stop being the puppet of desire

In the search to satisfy desire, we find ourselves with two trends: expansion and continence, extroversion and introversion.[4] In expansion, desire surfaces and grows, seeking satisfaction. It generates the dynamism of search and opening. When desire invades the soul and the soul cannot contain it, it becomes something destructive and devastating, like the cancer that devours everything it finds in its way. That way it turns into a dependence that is transformed into an addiction, Addiction to sex, to drink, to abuse, to submission, to imposing, to power, to money, etc. Then, desire enslaves us. Desire is the boss and we, its servants, who work to satisfy it. We lose our inner sovereignty. We are the puppets of desire.

All the spiritual paths propose phases to contain desire and control the senses in order not to be distracted from the greater and more transcendent search, to not remain trapped in the limited and to not lose oneself in the search for a momentary pleasure. Renouncing implies setting out some limits that help to guide the self towards a direction beyond itself. This will permit the connection and relationship with the transcendent. It allows for the development of inner sovereignty in order to stop being the puppet of desire. It will open up the universe or that awareness that is not limited by the corporeal. To renounce is to detach oneself. Any decision implies a giving up of something and, therefore, a cost that has to be accepted. You embrace something and you let go of something else. On being in tune with the energy of life, one learns the art of taking and detaching, like breathing: with each breath we breathe in life; with each exhalation we let go, we detach, we empty ourselves. If we hang on to the air that we breathe and we don't want to let it go, it stays inside us and poisons us. Air closed inside us becomes toxic. On letting it go and emptying ourselves of it, we free ourselves in the trust of a new breath. We fill ourselves and empty ourselves to fill ourselves again. It is the law of life.

Rebuild your own image

The concept of oneself is destiny. The danger is that we might become prisoners of our negative image, that we let it dictate our actions.
Nathaniel Branden[5]

A key to getting beyond female neediness and toxic masculinity lies in rebuilding your own image. An image of yourself independent of cultural stereotypes of gender. This means unlearning what has been learned. To set aside your masks, your labels, what is expected of you. This way the path is made clearer. It consists of unlearning, letting go, knowing and building.

Each woman, like each man, has to know what is good and what is bad for her or for him. What brings you closer to wholeness and what empties you. What connects you to your being and what disconnects you from the essential. To have your own criteria of value, and, from there, to value yourself. And to do so not only because of what happens in your emotional world, but rather because of the totality of your world. To have a complete image of being.

It is about knowing the eternal femininity and masculinity and your innate qualities, connecting with them and being them, living them, sharing them. Re-finding your axis, your backbone, in yourself and not looking for it in another. That way you rebuild your own image in the essence of your being.

Love yourself

When you have self-esteem, you feel secure. You belong to yourself and you trust.

Others can help you in your self-esteem but in the end loving yourself depends on you. That is why it is important to pay attention in relation to the group. Hence Branden puts to us the question:

Is not the physical and mental security of being integrated into a group a form of self-esteem? Does not the validation and support of the group give room to the experience of true personal worth? The error here lies in identifying any sensation of security or comfort with self-esteem. Conformity is not personal efficiency; popularity is not self-respect. Whatever its gratifications, the feeling of belonging to a group is not the same as the trust in my mind or the ability to be in control of life's challenges. The fact that others appreciate me does not guarantee that I will respect myself. (...) Poor self-esteem reduces the capacity for satisfaction.[6]

Again Branden states:

> The fact that we receive praise does not help us to create self-esteem. Neither is it created by erudition, material possessions, marriage, paternity, philanthropic efforts, sexual conquests or a face-lift. These things sometimes make us feel temporarily better or more comfortable in particular situations. But comfort is not self-esteem. The tragedy of many people's lives is that they look for self-esteem in different directions that are not their own and, therefore, fail in their search. Self-esteem is better understood as a spiritual achievement, as victory in the development of awareness.[7]

With break-ups, we often lose our self-esteem. The suffering that you go through in the situations when your husband or your partner leaves you is not only pain due to the loss of the other. As well as the loss, the woman feels that she is nobody, that she is worth nothing. You feel rejected. The man or woman you had committed yourself to has decided that this 'so great' other man or other girl is worth more than you, and you end up coming to the conclusion that you are not worth anything. A very deep wound is opened up, because your self-esteem, your value, disappears. You feel cast aside, excluded, separated. Remember the agreement: don't create suppositions. Don't suppose that because the other leaves you, you are worth less.

Achievements

As women we tend to be very critical of ourselves. Even when we are physically fine, we see ourselves as fat. When we work professionally, we diminish our achievements. Always the doubt in oneself remains: am I doing it right? Should I do it in another way to please him more, to be better, so that they like me more, etc? Isn't this a stupidity? Perhaps I had better keep quiet, better not to do it? Branden reminds us: 'If my objective is to prove that I am "enough", the project is prolonged infinitely.'

'Women have to be twice as good to get half of what men get,' says Agnes McPhail.

Many men base their self-esteem on what they have and on their achievements. If they lose what they have, if they lose their position, role, post or privileges, their self-esteem collapses. They have identified their being and their value with having. If they do not get what they want, they feel that their value goes down. They have been educated to triumph based on having and achieving. Getting back your intrinsic value, independently of your achievements and your possessions, will help you to love yourself as a human being. When you love yourself for what you are, you invite love into your life, in such a way that it flows like a river down each vein of your being.

Beauty

The beauty myth fosters low self-esteem and self-despising. Sometimes it even permits abuse. When you want to be loved but you live with the belief that you are not pretty, slim or thin enough, the situation can come to cause you eating disorders.

True beauty is in the soul. The soul is beautiful. If you root yourself in your being, you allow your beauty to shine with your virtues, values and talents. Then your eyes shine. Beauty is thera-peutic and supposes a balm for the emotions. Piero Ferrucci explains that 'when beauty fills us, even if only for an instant, all anguish, fear, sadness or wounds disappear, or at least are seen differently'.[8]

Goethe advised that 'every person should listen daily to a little delicate music, read a bit of good poetry and see a beautiful painting. That way the worries of daily life would not destroy the sense of beauty that God has planted in the human soul'.[9]

Value yourself

You have to learn to value yourself for what happens in the totality of your personal, relationship and professional world, not only in the love relationship. If a boyfriend has left you it's not the end of the world. You have a job that works for you, where possibly you are very valued and you earn money. As well, you have friends that love you or children that love you, or you are happy when traveling around the world or swimming in the sea.

You have at your disposal a series of elements that allow you to see that your being is not only of value if you are loved, but that, as a person, you have a whole range of things that enable you to value yourself. Being loved or not is a key piece, because it is as if the whole comes together and gives you an axis. But, in reality, if this axis is lost, there are many pieces left that you can put together because you are the axis. The problem lies in what I wrote about at the beginning of the book: love is the opium of women.

A lack of trust affects low self-esteem and vice versa. One doesn't have faith in oneself to be able to deal with whatever might come, and thus there is fear of change, of uncertainty, of the unknown. Your vulnerability takes over in you and your inner power remains dormant. 'Brilliant people with a low level of self-esteem act against their own interests every day,' says Branden.

Trust that good actions bring good returns. Cultivate positive thinking inside you; when you cleanse your heart of bitterness, then you get back trust and faith in yourself. Out of self-confidence and faith in yourself, you become the one who shines from the inside out. Like a Goddess who is beautiful on the inside and radiates her beauty full of the colors of the virtues and strengths. You go from lacking something to the gift. When you give yourself to the other, your self-esteem and your value grow.

Connect to your inner power

Thanks to the inner strength that throbs inside each one of us, we survive adversity and difficult circumstances. In periods of crisis, depression and disappointment, this inner strength helps us to surmount them. Our capacity to overcome critical or catastrophic situations is extraordinary. We have a great potential that seems to awaken in those circumstances.

The question is: what happens to this capacity when things are going more or less well, in the day to day? For what, when and where, do we use the potential that we have within? Does it perhaps only awaken when we face difficulties? It seems that when we are in 'the normality' of the day to day, we become careless and lazy, we lose our mental clarity and are weakened; then we complain, criticize and feel sorry for ourselves. Our capacity to live in wholeness, and not allow ourselves to be beaten by influences that weaken us, is atrophied.

Rabindranath Tagore reminds us:

Life is a river.
You are the boat that flows on the river.
If you let the water of life
Into your boat,
You will sink in the river.

When situations influence you and enter into your being, you no longer control your boat, you lose direction or you sink. Your thoughts are weakened and your feelings are of panic or suffocation. Your mind is triggered and you can't stop worrying. You get distracted and your vitality is dissipated. Your attention wanders and your energy is dispersed.

On the one hand, it is a matter of controlling your thoughts, being clear in your decisions and not letting yourself be ruled by your unhealthy habits. On the other hand, your inner power lies in not thinking one thing, feeling another, and finally, doing something else. Listen to your conscience, since it is the steering wheel of your life. If you listen to it, your decisions will be based on what upholds your integrity and your strength. That way, with your actions you will be able to express all your potential through helping yourself and others. When you act out of a clear vision, with self-esteem, trust and serenity, you have the ability to carry out your aims successfully. On so doing, you will feel satisfied.

When, on the contrary, what you do is not what you think or say, your words lose strength. When a father tells his son not to do something, but he himself does it, those words have no strength, given that they are not transmitted with the power of example. The son listens to the father's advice but sees that he himself does not follow it. This plants a doubt in him: why does he give me this advice, but he himself not do it?

The lack of integrity between what you think, say and do brings about a loss of power in your action, a lack of coherence and a diminishing of trust. What happens is that sometimes your conscience tells you to go in one direction but your beliefs, your fears and your habits lead you in another; then, who rules? The conscience that is nourished by your values, or your habits? At that moment you have to ask yourself: what do I really want? Listen to the voice of your heart, the center of your being. That way you will connect to your inner wisdom and your innate strength which will help you to overcome the habit.

Sometimes it is not your habits that influence you, but others. You trust more in what they say to you than in your own conscience and you act out of wanting to please the other, going against what you believe you have to do. The result is that your action does not carry the strength of all your being and its impact is reduced or lost altogether. You decide and act influenced by others and you want to please them, so you have expectations, you hope for their approval and pleasure. And when you are not happy with the other's response, you get angry, thus losing your inner peace and your energy.

You end up feeling like a puppet of circumstances and of others, or of your habits and your fears. For example, when you are irritated you think it is because this person is acting in such a way; you are in a bad mood because the weather is as it is; because the house has a crack in the ceiling; because the painter hasn't come; because the car won't start; because of this or that. So you are always complaining and frustrated. But who is responsible for your frustration? The weather, the car, the painter, the house—or are you responsible for what you do and how you respond to what happens? Stop being a victim and take your responsibility fully on board.

You choose how to respond to the stimuli that others and circumstances present. Recognize that you are responsible for your thoughts, words and actions. This is the initial base for recovering all your inner power. 'The greatest victory is the one you win over yourself,' Buddha told us. Live in harmony with what you think, with what you say and what you do. To do so, you have to be in ongoing contact with your inner strengths, with your capacity to see, to realize, to discern, to choose and to decide.

What is more, if you want to survive in peace the times of turbulence and changes we are living through, you should strengthen values such as tolerance, acceptance and flexibility, and meditate in order to think less, think better and think higher. That is, you should have thoughts with meaning and quality. In meditation, you connect to your inner wisdom, you get your clarity back and you find serenity.

Attention

Be attentive to the direction that the essential desire points you in, what you, the being, really long for, your deepest dream. This attention allows you to discern at each moment the quality of your dependent needs, of your searches and the way to satisfy them.

Being in a state of alertness and attention, without judging, condemning or blaming, accepting what is as it is, helps you to keep a clear vision. Being attentive to how you think, speak and behave widens your perception of what is and what you transmit.

In one of the weekly visits to the master, the disciple left, as was his custom, his sandals outside the door, and entered barefoot to meet him again. On this occasion, the master asked him where he had left the sandals: to the right or the left of the door. The disciple, surprised, answered that he didn't know. The master told him that this was a sign that he had not focused on the meditation well, since good meditation helps you to be attentive. He explained that if you do not pay attention to each action, allowing the mind to wander while acting, then you do not know where you have left the handkerchief, the keys, or, in this case, the sandals. This means your inner power is dispersed and you waste time looking for things; you lose energy and clarity because you weren't paying attention.

Sometimes you think 'I am going to do this', then another thought comes, and another. Hours pass before you realize: 'Oh, I was going to do that and I haven't done it!' You had that thought, but why didn't you do it? You didn't have concentration, clarity or focus; you had a long succession of thoughts, one after the other, and very quickly. Then you go from one task to another and you leave things half done, unfinished. Your to-do list becomes endless and disordered; disorganization and carelessness increase in your life. What is more, if you do something without being sure that you want to do it, doubting and afraid of failing, whatever you do won't have any force.

If your mind thinks too quickly and one thought crashes into another, your intellect hesitates and doesn't make a decision. If your past conditions you and blocks you, and if your habits lead you to worry without ceasing, your boat will sink again and again in the circumstances around you. You will lose the way and you will become distant from your essential desire.

To avoid this happening, you should get back your inner power, be alert and pay attention. Don't allow situations to carry you away and, slowly, to destroy your calm, or sink you into a river of worries.

Care for yourself and find calm

Only one thing matters: that nothing really matters, except maintaining the serenity of the mind and of one's speaking. Only serenity safeguards dignity.
Anthony Strano

The person whose spirit is free controls their mind, directs their thought, and keeps their attention centered. Their heart is at peace, radiating positive energy, and the energy of love. Not the physical heart that pumps the blood and makes it circulate, but rather the heart that is in the consciousness: the heart of the soul.

It seems that many have distanced themselves from their heart to install themselves in the mind. On turning the mind into our residence, we stay busy, filling it with preoccupations, anxiety, frustrations, annoyance and endless thoughts that wind us up and make us react. That way, little by little, we bury our true heart, the heart of the spirit.

Thoughts turn into a fog that prevents us from seeing and feeling with clarity. As these habits of thinking, of having a busy and reactive mind, very quickly get stronger, our heart empties and remains hungry for the fresh air of love. We lose calm.

To this is added the fact that often you are not kind to the mind. You force it with unnecessary thoughts and generate a jungle of chaotic thoughts instead of harmonious thoughts that grow a garden of fragrant flowers in your mind, beautiful, and full of color. You put pressure on the mind with your desires: I want this or I want to be like someone else. You begin by liking it, then you desire it and want it, you start needing it, next you start depending on it until it turns into an addiction. Throughout the process, your mind has been very pressured and stressed.

The stress is telling you that you have to change something. Thinking that stress is normal, that a bit of tension is fine, is a clear way of avoiding the inner work of self-responsibility and it is the sign of lazy thinking. It is not to be aware of the mental, emotional and physical wear and tear that stress causes you.

Fear, anxiety and worries generate a stress that paralyzes or distorts your ability to work out appropriate and efficient responses. A mind under pressure and with thoughts bumping into each other is less efficient. To find your inner power, practice calm. The mind is more creative when it is at inner peace; this is your personal power. How many times have your best ideas come into your mind while you were watering the plants, in the shower, walking or about to fall asleep? At those moments, your mind wasn't under pressure, and in that space of calm the brilliant idea surfaces. Like when Sir Isaac Newton saw an apple fall from the tree and had an 'aha!' moment. This is it!

You can receive physical treatments, therapies and use relaxation methods that will relieve some symptoms of stress, but they won't change your way of thinking nor the habits that cause you to feel stressed.

The cause of stress does not lie in what you do nor when you do it; what causes it is your way of thinking, perceiving and believing. Depending on your perception, you get more or less stressed. Your stress is directly proportional to your perception of reality.

You can choose positive perceptions and create constructive and healthy feelings. Or you can continue trapped in your habits of negative or lazy thoughts. It is a question of changing the perception and freeing yourself of the beliefs they bring about.

Learn to control your thoughts and feelings and fill them with calm and clarity. To overcome stress, you should take responsibility for how you are, think and feel. To do so, the first step is to stop, look inside you and listen. Take the pulse of what you think and incorporate the power of silence. In this way the mind will relax and work with greater concentration and freedom in the creative process. You will learn to let go, to accept and to stop putting up resistance. These attitudes are key to not getting stressed.

Learn to create an inner space in which you can find calm. In the calm, you make friends with the silence, with yourself and with God. When you are friends with the three of them, then you are friends with others and with the universe. Having turned your mind and your being into your friend, you find yourself at peace with yourself. Your inner dialogue provides you with energy and vitality; it keeps you serene and patient.

Most people avoid being calm, flee from silence and quietness. Watch yourself and realize how you avoid stopping, calming yourself, reconnecting to yourself in the quietness. What are you afraid of?

Our inner state depends on the relationship that we establish between heart and mind: it might be a path where dissatisfaction and suffering prevail, or a path that you undertake tranquilly, learning, and with the peace that is generated by acting with the wisdom of spiritual and emotional intelligence.

If you really meditate, if you truly enter into silence, wholeness will come to you. In meditation, in the inner silence, you will understand. Understanding is the light that helps you to see the steps that you should take. Out of wholeness, you give yourself to the other so that he or she might also re-find their wholeness.

In the silence you can come to experience a great interconnection. You are filled, you feel nourished and enriched. You give thanks. You savor the experience. Power arises in you that makes you go on to the next state: the expression of your wholeness, where transforming spaces are created.

Awakening

Even when we are awake and aware of the world that surrounds us, it is as if we were asleep and incapable of seeing the world as it is. We cannot see others as they really are and we are unable to see events in their true light. We see, we perceive and we interpret reality. Our intellect perceives the world and interprets it according to our beliefs and past experiences. If we learn to believe that we are bodies and not souls, that our emotions are caused by others, and that the world evolves in a positive and progressive way, those beliefs will influence our vision, perception and interpretation of other people's behavior, situations and world events in a particular way. Our thoughts, emotions and behavior respond to this. Each one of these beliefs is wrong. Check it.

In essence, we have our eyes closed in the face of these truths; that is why we pass through life asleep and don't even know it. As a result of wrong convictions, some form of suffering or pain will arise on an intimate level, but you will put up with that pain, believing it to be something normal. Only when the suffering becomes very intense do you recognize that you have to do something.

To achieve a real and lasting transformation, only the practice of meditation and the in-depth study of the knowledge of the truths about the identity of being will heal, in the last instance, your emotional, mental and spiritual pain.

We all have the capacity to watch instead of sleep, to awaken to the reality of the spirit (which we are made of) and offer our invigorating power to those who remain asleep around us. When one awakens spiritually, so too does their intuition, the voice of their soul, the voice that says it really wants to free itself of the fears and ties. Normally that voice is stifled by an intellect that is constantly analyzing, criticizing, blaming and judging wrongly. It remains stifled by a mind that is dispersed and feels controlled by fear.

On awakening to the spirit, you dissipate the fear that your relationships with others causes you and you welcome in love in its place. In reality, no one can hurt you. On extending your forgiveness to those who treat you with little consideration, you accumulate the spiritual merit of generating good karma and you receive many blessings. The blessings emanate from a heart that is awake, and awaken all those who receive them.

Anthony de Mello says to us about awakening: 'If you manage to keep your spirit free of obstacles and your senses open, you will begin to perceive things as they are, and to establish a mutual interaction with reality and you will be captivated by the harmony of the universe. Then you will understand what God is, because finally you will have understood what love is.'[10]

We should increase our awareness of our capacity to live with greater wholeness. We live in a state of ignorance, of lethargy.

There are habits, seductively pleasurable attachments, that prevent you from reaching your potential. Then you live controlled by those habits that keep you in a state of dormancy. Wake up and live in your inner power.

Chapter 8

Live In Your Inner Power

The Goddesses

When a woman is reborn brimming over with freedom, she breaks the circle that condemns her.
Mar Correa[1]

The moment has come to change the paradigm of the patriarchy that fuels the dependent and submissive woman. Many women still find that devoting themselves to empowering themselves, and the world, is less interesting than devoting themselves to a marvellous man, because culturally we have been programmed that way.

Let's detach ourselves. Let's free ourselves of the cultural influences and unfold all our potential. Let's feel ourselves Goddesses who can act on the world and change it. Influence the ways of the world and transform them. Authentic leaders, beautiful, powerful, loving, tolerant, compassionate, generous, delicate and strong. Powerful, with a power associated with their own value and talent, and not that of the system or position in a professional hierarchy. A power that does not impose itself, but rather surfaces out of our authenticity. A power that frees us of the need for the approval of the other.

Women who emanate humility, wisdom, love and power, and who subscribe to the need to reinvent the male gender, helping men to realize that they do not represent a threat and therefore, they can let go of all their pretensions of control and being in charge.

The Goddesses have divine authority. It is not a religious authority that imposes, represses, forces and punishes. Their authority emanates from their knowledge, their experience and their transparency, which reflects the divine. The rainbow of God: their powers and their virtues. They are the Goddesses of discernment (Gayatri) and of decision with wisdom (Sarasvati), of the power to confront (Kali), of acceptance (Santosh), of tolerance (Jagadamba or the Mother of the world). Goddesses with the power of letting go (Durga), of withdrawal (Parvati) and of co-operating, or Goddesses of abundance and richness (Lakshmi).

They are independent Goddesses but with connected spirits. They work together on a higher level of thought and being. In this way, they embrace the world without suffocating it. They take strength and nourishment from their being, from the source, and not from the effects of their actions. The Goddess is the woman connected to her original qualities: purity, power, peace, happiness, love and truth.

When we feel that longing to return there, we realize that we have forgotten where to look. We forget that the place where everything begins resides in the invisible: the inner world of thoughts and feelings. Everything arises first in the sphere of thought and the imagination.

It is not possible to achieve one's own autonomy without first understanding why we no longer have that power that we vaguely remember having had. It is necessary to understand where and how we lost it: to understand how to control our field of personal energy so that it is not contaminated with dependences or desires that distance us from our essence.

Eckhart Tolle explains to us that 'the suppression of the feminine principle, especially in the last two thousand years, has allowed the ego to achieve absolute supremacy in the collective human psyche. Although women, naturally, have egos, the ego can take root and grow more easily in the male form than in the feminine. This is due to the fact that women are less identified with the mind than men. They are more in contact with the inner body and the intelligence of the organism, where the intuitive faculties originate. The feminine form is less rigidly enclosed than the masculine, it is more open and more sensitive to other forms of life, and more in tune with the natural world.' In many ancient pre-Christian civilizations, like the Sumerian, the Egyptian and the Celtic, women were respected and the feminine principle was not feared but revered. What made men suddenly feel threatened by women? Tolle says that it was the ego that was developing in the men. It knew that it could only achieve full control of our planet through the male form, and to achieve this it had to leave the feminine without power. With time the ego also took control of women.

'Now we are in a situation where the suppression of women has been taken on board by most women. The sacred feminine principle, on being repressed, is felt by many women as emotional pain.

'But now things are changing rapidly. As more people are becoming conscious, the ego is losing its power over the human mind. Since the ego was never so deeply rooted in women, it is losing its control over women more quickly than over men'.[2]

Let us see how to transcend the ego through opening our awareness.

Opening the awareness: communion with the origin

There is no more important task for the human being than that of connecting with one's own soul and awakening the energy contained there in order to unfold the potential it shelters. In order to do this, all spiritual traditions are proponents of the need to transcend the ego.

Ramana Maharshi, a Hindu mystic of the last century, says: 'Eliminate the ego and ignorance disappears. Ignorance belongs to the ego. Why do you think about the ego and suffer? An ignorance that consists of the forgetting of the soul. If you know the soul there will no longer be darkness, nor ignorance, nor misery'.

The ego hardens us and prevents us from recognising ourselves as who we truly are. The needs of the ego keep us trapped and centred on ourselves, and we allow ourselves to be guided by our lesser nature. It is a question of un-identifying ourselves from the ego in order to let go and free ourselves of the passionate desire and the compulsive forces that trap the soul in the bodily dimension and do not allow it to reach the transcendent dimension.

All the spiritual paths say to us that we should empty or transform the 'I' radically, and that way, the shadows that surround it will disappear. The extinction of the ego does not bring with it the annihilation of the deepest self. On the contrary, it allows its manifestation. It is a matter of transcending the limits of one's own psyche: ideas, projects, securities, attachments and beliefs that are still references of the limited self. In this way, we will achieve the transformation of the self-centred impulses of the ego into creative capacities and generators of life and communion.

On transcending the ego, our soul is conscious of a wider reality than the one that can be perceived through the senses. You realise what is really important. **You stop reacting out of a defensive posture** and you show yourself without fears such as you are. The awareness is opened to new perspectives and you access the deepest knowledge of the self.

As the reference of the ego is transcended, the person starts to acquire a knowledge that is no longer centred on one's own physiological and psychological needs. As the awareness is awoken, the limits of the ego are discovered, **the sacralization of one's own being is discovered** and one learns to transcend it in order to enter into connection with the wisdom that unites us all and with the Whole. Thus does the deepest self manifest itself with all its creative capacity, generator of life and of communion.

'If the grain of wheat does not die when it falls to the ground, it remains alone, but if it dies, it bears much fruit.' John 12, 24

Renouncing the limited self means to **go through various states of 'deaths'** in which one is emptied of what they contained, and is completely flooded, not with something that has to be defended like before out of the strength of the ego, but rather with the awareness that this self has turned into a pure receptacle: the heart of the soul, the space dislodged by the ego. When one reaches this place, one reaches **the communion with the origin**, with the Whole and with all people.

In that state, day to day situations stop affecting you negatively, you remain stable and in harmony and you feel serenity. Your thoughts are precise, they do not run away like a wild horse; rather, you control them. **You recognise what is authentic** and you do not allow yourself to be impressed by the illusions of falsity and ignorance. You free yourself from anger, rage, bitterness and greed. This allows you to be more generous. Out of clarity, before acting you become aware of the consequences of your acts and you do not allow yourself to be carried away by the impulse of desire or outside influences; rather you act out of a discernment based on innate wisdom and on the knowledge of the law of cause and effect.

To **leave ignorance behind**, all the spiritual paths suggest to us that we resort assiduously to prayer or to meditation, where the self reaches the soul and opens itself to the possibility of a transcendent connection.

In the silence, you calm the voice and noise of the ego. In meditation you dissolve it and empty yourself. In contemplation, the consciousness and intuition connected to the innate wisdom are awakened: there individuality opens itself to the Whole.

The flow of energy

The Goddess is aware that, if she were to fight against the

existing system, what she would do is give her power over to it. She is aware that the system of domination has to do with impotence, with working with limited quantities of energy. This happens when you work only with the energy provided by your ego, your body and the achievements of your actions. When you work out of the awareness of lack and shortage, your energy is limited. That system sets out from a base that believes and affirms that only a certain amount of energy exists and that because of this we should take power away from others, since we do not know where or how to replenish ourselves.

All that we take from a source within the system keeps us in the system and, therefore, we should return it to the system. That is why we keep going in a circle, going round and round the same things without changing the quality of the energy nor of what we bring to the system.

To work with abundant energy is to be aware that **you are a channel**, an instrument, abeing connected to the Whole and to the universe. Drinking from the divine, spiritual and transcendent energy brings you the capacity to **change the system together with others** who are also aware that now we should act together out of an awakened consciousness, without limits.

Tolle reminds us that 'without the deterioration caused by the egotistical dysfunction, our intelligence enters fully into tune with the expansive cycle of universal intelligence and its impulse to create. We become conscious participants in the creation of form. It is not us who creates, but the universal intelligence, which **creates through us**. We do not identify ourselves with what we create and that way we do not lose ourselves in what we do. We are learning that the act of creation can mean energy of enormous intensity, but that this is not "hard work" or overwhelming. We have to understand the difference between stress and intensity. Fighting or stress is a sign that the ego has returned, as too are negative reactions when we find obstacles.

The only actions that do not provoke opposite reactions are those aimed at the good of all. They are inclusive, not excluding. They join, they do not separate'.[3]

The Goddesses have access to the abundant and unlimited quantities of energy that are beyond the limits of the prevailing system, which means they become beings full of possibility and power. They have modified their limited identity and their sense of being, and thus managed to displace the limits and eliminate the boundary lines. They have transcended the ego-character, the personage, the limited self.

In this state, you are aware that your being exists without the interpretation, praise, defamation or judgement of anyone else. You are because you are. We call this 'internal reference'. You do not identify yourself any more with a wide collective, with rules that define how women and men should be, nor do you try to manipulate in order to achieve power within the patriarchal family structure. Those would be your external references. You act out of your internal references without needing to reject the system. You accept it to transform it.

The Goddess rules over all the intelligences, including spiritual intelligence, the intelligence against adversity (resilience), creative intelligence and divine intelligence: wisdom. That would be a subject for another book.

The passion of a Goddess leads her to a transcendent love. It creates transcendence. It is not a suffocating love, nor a love that stays between you and I, but rather a love that has influence on the world, that has a transforming presence and impact. Thus, she is aware that the mind —in its original state— is not gendered, in the same way that the soul —in its eternal consciousness— transcends gender. It is an enthralling possibility.

On a personal level, let us reinvent love in relationships, conscious of the fact that fusion is only momentary, luckily for us. If the fusion was forever, when someone dies, we would have to die with that person, as is the case in the tradition whereby widows immolate themselves with to their dead husband, the *sati*. It is not precisely a question of a death out of fusion but rather a death out of despair.

Sati is an example of a Hindu tradition that takes away power from the woman on establishing that her husband will always be her God. On his dying, she often is abandoned to her luck: the relatives of her husband can take her children away from her to educate them in the father's name, and expel the wife from the home even though she has no way of earning her living. In such cases, rarely will she be taken back into her own parents' home, who have often paid a significant dowry to be free of their responsibility towards her. Depending on which place and culture of India it is, woman today still does not have access to paid work. Thus, the most natural thing is that she decide 'to go away' together with her deceased husband. In other cases, she goes to a refuge for widows, where she ekes out a living through prostitution. That is not a love of fusion. It is a sacrifice that could be avoided.

Let us return to the subject of the Goddesses. The Goddesses allow the other to be. They generate spaces of freedom, of forgiveness and forgetting, of reconciliation. They help the other, but without rescuing them, without feeling them to be a victim. The consciousness of the rescuer would deprive them of their power. In this way, they endow the other with autonomy without losing their own energy, without trying to dominate or possess the other.

The Goddess knows herself. She is strong, but not aggressive. She is trustworthy and trusting. The Goddess is free, she doesn't have limiting expectations. She thinks about the best for the other, and gives it to them. She is connected to the divine source and she feels whole. She radiates like the sun. She does not empty. Energy flows through her, it does not stagnate, it does not get blocked. She does not live only from her own energy. She reaches to the universal, divine and supreme energy. The Goddess is love.

Chapter 9

Creating and Constructing a New Paradigm Together

Love is something dangerous; it brings with it the only revolution that gives complete happiness.[1]
Jiddu Krishnamurti

'Those that wish to create a new culture, a new society, a new state of things, should first understand themselves. The important thing is that each should understand themselves in their relationship with the other.'[2] That way we will be able to co-operate out of a shared living that will be a 'we' and not a sum of 'I's.

Shahrukh Husain writes about the creation of the Golden Age and explains to us that it is possible that a society around the religion of the Goddess existed.[3] The said society did not concern itself with conquest or domination. The architectural remains found do not show defensive structures, like fortresses. The one hundred and fifty paintings found in the area do not show scenes of violence. They led a peaceful lifestyle. Their organization was centered on peaceful interactions and artistic development. These statements are supported by the finding of the civilization of Höyük Zatal, in Turkey.

'The hope exists,' Shahrukh continues to explain, 'that the ideal of the Goddess might unite women and help them to create, together with men, a less materialistic society, in which humanity cohabits peacefully.'

Reinventing ourselves
To collaborate in creating and constructing a new paradigm, first you should be awake and see with clarity. Stop maintaining the

old so that the new can be born. Be aware of the impact that your thoughts, your beliefs and your vision have on your life and on your relationships. It is an awakening that means being responsible and being aware of the need to co-operate, show solidarity and live with values, having a broad and global vision that includes the spiritual dimension.

So, both as women and men, we should reinvent our life. Reinventing it means changing our pattern of behavior and acting out of another space. Acting out of generosity and no longer being needy, attached and dependent women.

Let us be the deities of today and tomorrow. That is, Goddesses and Gods who can act on the world and change it from the flow of unlimited love that is in our reach.

We find it very difficult because, on the one hand, we don't let go of dependences or cultural stereotypes and, on the other, we still haven't connected to the experience of authentic power. The power for the creation of life, not for destruction in a competition.

A woman deeply rooted in her essence does not destroy what she creates. If women gain access to that space in which they can lead and do not allow themselves to be influenced by toxic masculinity, violence will be reduced. A moment will come in which it will make no sense and will disappear.

When we see the situation of the world, many of us want to serve it. But when our minds are affected by the global situation, really we cannot serve. A mind full of anger or sadness, of complaints and laments, cannot serve in order to generate a transformation with real impact.

In capitalism, the outside world became more and more of a male world, and the interior was defined as a feminine space. We should all cultivate our inner space and go out into the world to share out wisdom, compassion, solidarity, love, tolerance, acceptance, understanding and unification. We are aware of the fact that we cannot give to others when we feel weakened by the heaviness of the world, and by the atmosphere of a tired world. We can only give to others when we have got our spiritual power back.

A mind capable of healing the world

For the boat to reach its destiny, the water should stay out of the boat. For our minds to be able to serve, the atmosphere of the world should stay outside of our minds. It should not happen that the outside toxic atmosphere penetrates the boat of our mind, but rather the opposite, that the vibrations of a powerful and clean mind might influence the outside atmosphere, strengthening those who live in the world.

To have a mind that is capable of healing the world, first we should heal ourselves, cultivating healing powers such as hope, harmony, compassion, forgiveness, tolerance and respect.

When we fill ourselves with the power of spirituality, we emanate it continuously. We create each thought and each feeling with an intention that is to the good, and is of service. When the world has enough people with a mind of this kind, then the new earth, the Golden Age, will come, bringing peace and light to the world.

Living in the being

The deities live in the being and thus facilitate the transition from the culture of having to the culture of being. It is a culture in which one does not diminish the other to strengthen oneself, nor judge them superior or inferior. They create methods to prepare everyone, returning hope to each one of them. This preparation is a spiritual empowerment. It requires of us that we practice the art and science of silence, from where we connect to our intuition, our inner guide that is the driving force of transforming creativity.

Women deeply rooted in their eternal identity, that is, the Goddesses, generate spaces of trust in which men allow women to set out new rules, even if it is in the territory that they consider to belong to them. The Goddesses want to have men at their side, not in front of them, because, in these moments of crisis, there are far more crucial battles to uphold. Battles that, if we do not defeat them, will put our continuation into question: global warming, the consumption of water, hunger, child labor, wars…

When as men and women we live in the essential being, we will work together as partners in the creation of a new world. We will allow the old structures built by the ego to fall for good and we will make way for a new creation.

A creative working world

In this way we will have the inner power necessary to change the mandates that make up gender identity in our culture. Until they are transformed, compassion, fraternity, transcendence, spirituality, humanism, and a space for otherness will not enter into the working world.

The Goddesses and Gods will change the paradigm of work as a means of production through generating spaces of creativity, as a form of deep connection, as a territory of solidarity, as an opening to transcendence. A transcendence that does not diminish productivity, but rather improves it with quality, integrity and equanimity.

A new vision

As women and men stabilize themselves in this awareness, let us see this new world. To do so, we can ask ourselves:

What would relationships be like?
How would education be given?
How would we design a village or town?
What would the houses be like, the car parks, the avenues, the walks, the parks, the streets, the lighting, the benches to sit on in the street?

How would we share talent and creativity?
How would we govern?
What would communications be like?

Let us visualize. Let us root ourselves in our inner power, generate a vision, believe in it and share it in order to make it into a reality out of respect and co-operation.

Let us begin, as women, by ourselves: let us eradicate from inside us the burden of centuries that makes us feel that we are 'less' and let us sit on the immortal throne of our soul consciousness, the eternal being. The Goddesses teach that power is not lost if it is shared. This is the co-operation that is necessary. Let us create spaces of human enrichment, scenarios that are open to the service of the other and the planet, with all its inhabitants. Let us become reference points for a new leadership: inspiring, transforming, generous, welcoming, creative and brilliant.

The people that have awakened to this new form of essential being, without masks, with humility and personal power, without submission, with these new thoughts, feelings, attitudes and values, will join together in a harmonious way. In a natural way, they will unite to create a new culture, a new civilization.

There will be complementarity between different groups and people, not competition or jealousy. Neither victims nor aggressors; neither oppressed nor oppressors. We will be partners.

We will experience an equality of feeling: a feeling of love, generosity and unity. We will feel an equality of vision: a world in harmony, a just world. We will have one same purpose: a better world for 'all'.

This will come because each one will have carried out their real and transforming research in the laboratory of their life. With practice and experience, we will be on the same vibrational wave. We will live out deep faith in non-violence as a lifestyle. We will share the same aims and values. We will pursue a similar lifestyle, based on respect for all living beings.

We will understand each other without having to explain things a hundred times. We will experience a practical telepathy: being able to communicate our thoughts and understand each other. Real collective telepathy. Our antennae, our consciousnesses and minds will be clean of unnecessary thoughts and upsetting noises.

We will be a group of people working together, with a collective consciousness, to create a new world. Consciousness here on Earth, centered in time and space.

Creating this new world depends on me, you and everyone. Get going. When you change, the world will change.

Bibliography

Bauman, Zygmunt, *Liquid Love: On the Frailty of Human Bonds*, Polity, Cambridge, 2003.

Branden, Nathaniel, *The Six Pillars of Self-Esteem: The Definitive Work on Self-Esteem by the Leading Pioneer in the Field*, Bantam, 1995.

Bristow, Wendy, *Single and Loving It: How to Be Happy and Whole When There Is No Other Half*, Thorsons, 2000.

Canfield Fisher, Dorothy, *Her Son's Wife*, Harcourt Brace, New York, 1926.

Castells, Manuel and Marina Subirats, *Mujeres y hombres, ¿un amor imposible?*, Alianza Editorial, Madrid, 2007.

Correa, Mar, *El príncipe azul no vive aquí. La nueva mujer y las nuevas familias*, RD Editores, Seville, 2007.

De Mello, Anthony, *Call to Love*, copyright: Gujarat Sahitya Prakash Anand, India, 1991.

Dispenza, Joe, *Evolve Your Brain: The Science of Changing Your Mind*, Deerfield, Florida, 2007.

Duna Mascetti, Manuela, *Diosas. La canción de Eva*, Malsinet, Barcelona, 2008.

Dyer, Wayne W., *Your Erroneous Zones*, Funk and Wagnalls, New York, 1976.

Eckhart, Maestro, *El fruto de la nada*, Siruela, Madrid, 2006.

Ferrucci, Piero, *Beauty and the Soul*, Penguin Group, USA, 2009.

Hanauer, Cathi, *The Bitch in the House*, Penguin Books, London, 2003.

Husain, Shahrukh, *The Goddess: Creation, Fertility and Abundance, The Sovereignty of Women, Myths and Archetypes*, Little Brown and Co, London, 1997.

Jakayar, Pupul, *Krishnamurti: A Biography*, Harper and Row, San Francisco, 1986.

Jericó, Pilar, *Héroes cotidianos. Descubre el valor que llevas dentro,* Planeta, Barcelona, 2010.

Krishnamurti, Jiddu, *On Relationship,* Harper, San Francisco, 1992.

Marina, José Antonio, *Aprender a convivir,* Ariel, Barcelona, 2006.

Melloni, Javier, *El deseo esencial,* Sal Terrae, Santander, 2009.

Pizzey, Erin, *Prone to Violence,* Bennett, Great Britain, 1982.

Ruiz, Miguel, *Los cuatro acuerdos: una guía práctica para la libertad personal,* Urano, Barcelona, 1998.

Sinay, Sergio, *La masculinidad tóxica. Un paradigma que enferma a la sociedad y amenaza a las personas,* Ediciones B, Buenos Aires, 2006.

Schellenbaum, Peter, *La herida de los no amados. El estigma de la falta de amor,* Editorial Ibis, Barcelona, 1993.

Strano, Anthony, *El arte de discernir,* Editorial Asociación Brahma Kumaris, Barcelona, 2009.

Subirana, Miriam, *Creativity to Reinvent Your Life: Reflections on Change, Intuition and Spiritual Alchemy,* O Books, UK, 2010.

__, *Dare to Live: Reflections on Fear, Courage and Wholeness,* O Books, UK, 2008.

—, *Live in Freedom: Reflections on Limits, Dreams and the Essential,* O Books, UK, 2009.

Tolle, Eckhart, *A New Earth: Awakening to Your Life's Purpose,* Penguin Books, UK, 2005.

Ward, Caroline, *The Four Faces of Woman: Restoring Your Authentic Power, Recovering Your Eternal Beauty,* O Books, 2008.

Wittenberg-Cox, Avivah and Alison Maitland, *Why Women Mean Business: Understanding the Emergence of our Next Economic Revolution,* Jossey-Bass, San Francisco, 2008.

Notes

Introduction

1. Manuel Castells and Marina Subirats, *Mujeres y hombres, ¿un amor imposible?*, Alianza Editorial, Madrid, 2007.

Chapter 1 The Context

1. La Sección Femenina de Falange de la JONS y la SF (1934–1959).
2. Medina, *Revista de la Sección Femenina*, 13 August 1944.
3. Wendy Bristow, *Single and Loving It: How to Be Happy and Whole When There Is No Other Half*, Thorsons, 2000.
4. Interview by Lluís Amiguet of Teresa Forcades in 'La Contra', *La Vanguardia*, 17 October 2007.
5. Mar Correa, *El príncipe azul no vive aquí. La nueva mujer y las nuevas familias*, RD Editores, Sevilla, 2007.
6. Source: http://www.cambrabcn.org/c/document_library.
7. Information taken from the article: 'Men for Equality: The Inner Male Revolution?' by Silvia Melero. Published in *21rs La revista cristiana de hoy*, March 2008. Websites of interest: www.ahige.org and www.stop- machismo.net.

Chapter 2 Neediness

1. The presentation of the book in Spanish by Miriam Subirana, *Creatividad para reinventar tu vida. Reflexiones sobre el cambio, la intuición y la alquimia espiritual*, RBA-Integral, Barcelona, 2009, took place on 26 May 2009, at FNAC Barcelona.
2. I deal with this subject in greater depth in my book *Live in Freedom: Reflections on Limits, Dreams and the Essential*, O Books, UK, 2009.
3. Javier Melloni has an excellent book with this title: *El deseo esencial*, Sal Terrae, Santander, 2009.
4. I shared a program about choosing between desires and

needs on 'L'Ofici de Viure', *Catalunya Ràdio*, with Josep Maria Fericgla. He said these words there.

5. Wendy Bristow, ibid.
6. Eckhart Tolle, *A New Earth: Awakening to Your Life's Purpose*, Penguin Books, UK, 2005.
7. Interview published in 'La Contra', *La Vanguardia*.
8. Sílvia Munt interviewed by Lluís Bonet in *La Vanguardia*, 12 June 2008. Munt is an actress and film director.
9. Dorothy Canfield Fisher, *Her Son's Wife*, Brace and Company, Virago, London, 1986.

Chapter 3 Toxic Masculinity
1. Some of the ideas in this section have been inspired by Sergio Sinay through his book *La masculinidad tóxica. Un paradigma que enferma a la sociedad y amenaza a las personas*, Ediciones B, Buenos Aires, 2006.
2. Data published by Sergio Sinay in his book.
3. Source: II Annual Report of the State Observatory of Violence against Women.
4. Source: Violence against Women in Judicial Statistics. Second term of 2009. www.observatorioviolencia.org/documentos.php.
5. Source: 'It's not just hitting. Lecture by immigrant women on gender violence', *Bembea: Estrategias contra el racismo y la xenofobia*, 2008.
6. Source: DGPNSD. Spanish Observatory of Drugs (OED). Report for 2007 www.pnsd.msc.es.
7. Source: '*Dones i Treball. Publicació estadística del Departament de Treball*', January 2008.
8. Nathaniel Branden, *The Six Pillars of Self-Esteem: The Definitive Work on Self-Esteem by the Leading Pioneer in the Field*, Bantam, 1995.
9. Eckhart Tolle, ibid.
10. Eckhart Tolle, ibid.

11. Sergio Sinay, ibid.
12. Sergio Sinay, ibid.
13. Course 'Facilitating processes of dialogue and efforts at mediation'. *Program to promote women peace-makers* (*Women Peace-Makers*). Folke Bernadotte Academy, Sandö, Sweden, December 2008.

Chapter 4 Relationships

1. Manuel Castells and Marina Subirats, ibid.
2. Javier Melloni, ibid.
3. Sergio Sinay, ibid.
4. Mar Correa, ibid.
5. Mar Correa, ibid.
6. Wayne W. Dyer, *Your Erroneous Zones*, Funk and Wagnalls, New York, 1976.
7. Blog: www.pilarjerico.com.
8. Mar Correa, ibid.
9. *Maya*, a word used in India referring to mirages, to falsity, what appears to be but is not.
10. Jiddu Krishnamurti, 'Lucky the man that is not', 'Letters to a Young Friend', published in Jakayar, Pupul's *Krishnamurti: A Biography*, Harper and Row, San Francisco, 1986.
11. Jiddu Krishnamurti, *On Relationship*, Harper, San Francisco, 1992.
12. Mar Correa, ibid.
13. Source: www.ine.es. Data from the census of 2001.
14. Source: www.idescat.cat.
15. Dispenza, Joe, *Evolve Your Brain: The Science of Changing Your Mind*, Deerfield, Florida, 2007.
16. In the book *Live in Freedom*, I deal widely with the subject of beliefs and their influence on all areas of our life.

Chapter 5 New Relationships

1. Wendy Bristow, ibid.

2. Jiddu Krishnamurti, ibid.
3. Sergio Sinay, ibid.
4. Nathaniel Branden, ibid.
5. Miguel Ruiz, *Los cuatro acuerdos: una guía práctica para la libertad personal*, Urano, Barcelona, 1998.

Chapter 6 Partners in Complementarity

1. Sergio Sinay, ibid.
2. Cited by Caroline Ward in *The Four Faces of Woman: Restoring Your Authentic Power, Recovering Your Eternal Beauty*, O Books, 2008.
3. Manuel Castells and Marina Subirats, ibid.
4. Sergio Sinay, ibid.
5. Sergio Sinay, ibid.

Chapter 7 Partners to Live in Wholeness

1. Javier Melloni, ibid.
2. Eckhart Tolle, ibid.
3. Anthony Strano, *Los cuatro movimientos naturales: el arte de discernir*, Editorial Asociación Brahma Kumaris, Barcelona, 2009.
4. Javier Melloni explains this in his book *El deseo esencial*.
5. Nathaniel Branden, ibid.
6. Nathaniel Branden, ibid.
7. Nathaniel Branden. ibid.
8. Piero Ferrucci, *Beauty and the Soul*, Penguin Group, USA, 2009.
9. Quote from Johann Wolfgang Von Goethe.
10. Anthony de Mello, *Call to Love*, copyright: Gujarat Sahitya Prakash Anand, India, 1991.

Chapter 8

1. Mar Correa, *ibid.*
2. Eckhart Tolle, *ibid.*

3.   Eckhart Tolle, *ibid*.

Chapter 9 Creating and Constructing a New Paradigm Together

1.   Pupul Jakayar, ibid.
2.   Jiddu Krishnamurti, ibid.
3.   Shahrukh Husain, *The Goddess: Creation, Fertility and Abundance, The Sovereignty of Women, Myths and Archetypes*, Little Brown and Co, London, 1997.

BOOKS

O is a symbol of the world, of oneness and unity. In different cultures it also means the "eye," symbolizing knowledge and insight. We aim to publish books that are accessible, constructive and that challenge accepted opinion, both that of academia and the "moral majority."

Our books are available in all good English language bookstores worldwide. If you don't see the book on the shelves ask the bookstore to order it for you, quoting the ISBN number and title. Alternatively you can order online (all major online retail sites carry our titles) or contact the distributor in the relevant country, listed on the copyright page.

See our website **www.o-books.net** for a full list of over 500 titles, growing by 100 a year.

And tune in to myspiritradio.com for our book review radio show, hosted by June-Elleni Laine, where you can listen to the authors discussing their books.